THE CONTEMPORARY PRAXIS
OF THE FANTASTIC
Borges and Cortázar

LATIN AMERICAN STUDIES
(VOL. 1)

GARLAND REFERENCE LIBRARY
OF THE HUMANITIES
(VOL. 1435)

LATIN AMERICAN STUDIES

General Editor: David William Foster

THE CONTEMPORARY PRAXIS
OF THE FANTASTIC
Borges and Cortázar

Julio Rodríguez-Luis

GARLAND PUBLISHING, INC. • NEW YORK & LONDON
1991

Library of Congress Cataloging-in-Publication Data

Rodríguez-Luis, Julio.
   The contemporary praxis of the fantastic : Borges and Cortázar /
Julio Rodríguez-Luis.
      p.   cm. — (Latin American studies (Garland) ; vol. 1)
(Garland reference library of the humanities ; vol. 1435)
   Includes bibliographical references and index.
   ISBN 0-8153-0101-4 (alk. paper)
   1. Borges, Jorge Luis, 1899–   —Criticism and interpretation.
2. Cortázar, Julio—Criticism and interpretation. 2. Fantastic
fiction, Spanish American—History and criticism. 4. Spanish
American fiction—20th century—History and criticism. I. Title.
II. Series. III. Series: Garland reference library of the
humanities ; vol. 1435.
PQ7797.B635Z9127   1991
863—dc20   91–23877
                                                      CIP

Printed on acid-free, 250-year-life paper
Manufactured in the United States of America

To my students in Binghamton and Berlin. The arguments that follow were, to a great extent, born out of our discussions about Cortázar and Borges. And to Judith Sumner, without whose invaluable help this book would have remained unpublished.

Table of Contents

Foreword

The work of Borges and Cortázar has been widely studied, often with great analytical and theoretical sophistication. Many, if not a majority, of the critics have approached the bulk of Borges' and Cortázar's stories as examples of the fantastic; some, even while studying those same works from different points of view, tend to assume that they are fantastic. This is due in part to the fact that the writers themselves, in prefaces and essays, have encouraged this characterization of their most famous texts.

Meanwhile, a critical discourse on fantastic literature considered as a genre or as a mode has been developing since at least the end of the sixties. Because Latin American literature is not yet fully part of the literary mainstream, the examples that critics choose to illustrate their investigations of the fantastic tend to be drawn mostly from French, English, American, and German literatures. Only exceptionally (Barrenechea) has there been an attempt to develop a theory of the fantastic centered on its Latin American practice. Rare too (Alazraki) has been any application of the theoretical analysis of the fantastic to the work of a Latin American author (Cortázar).

The purpose of this monograph is to study Borges' and Cortázar's stories *strictly* from the point of view of a theory of the fantastic, with the intention of determining with some certainty whether some of those stories are in fact fantastic narratives, and if so, in what specific manner and to what extent. In order to accomplish this task it seems necessary, before proceeding to the actual study of Borges' and Cortázar's stories, to begin with a brief review of the critical analysis of the fantastic. To my knowledge, no other overview of the theory of the fantastic, and especially none that takes into account its Latin American manifestations, is currently available.

I try to maintain my discussion of Borges' and Cortázar's stories within the frame provided by the analysis of the fantastic. It is inevitable, however, that when writing about texts as rich in meanings as those that are the object of this study, the critic will step, even if only briefly, into other areas of critical concern.

Neither when approaching the stories solely from the point of view of the fantastic nor when studying them from other angles does my study pretend to be exhaustive. My purpose is to determine which stories are fantastic, and that done, to explore the ways in which they function as fantastic narratives. Let me stress that this dual analysis has not been attempted so far.

The study of the stories as well as the review of the theory of the fantastic that precedes it both assume a certain degree of familiarity on the part of the reader with contemporary critical discourse and its terminology. Since this study is not addressed exclusively to the specialist in Latin American literature, it has seemed useful to provide brief summaries of the action of the stories under discussion. I have kept to a minimum references to the critical analyses of Borges' and Cortázar's works, especially when they do not touch on the main thrust of my study.

After discussing the relationship between the fantastic and magical realism, I will propose, on the basis of the discussion of critical theory and the analyses of texts that precede, a working definition of the fantastic. The very last section of the conclusion is devoted to exploring the role of the fantastic in contemporary fiction.

The Contemporary Praxis
of the Fantastic
Borges and Cortázar

Chapter One

Todorov and the Analysis of the Fantastic

The criticism of the fantastic—those narrative works characterized by the dominant role that fantasy plays in their plots—has undergone a very noticeable, even drastic change in the last two decades. The most conspicuous manifestation of that change is Tzvetan Todorov's 1970 study of the fantastic, *Introduction à la littérature fantastique*, a book whose impact on the critical appraisal of the literature it deals with has made it a classic. This does not mean that Todorov's positing of the fantastic as a full (though already extinct) genre or his analysis of its structure has been universally accepted. On the contrary, both have been criticized and attacked; but this criticism has in fact served to underscore the importance of the *Introduction*.

Prior to 1970 our ideas regarding the fantastic were, notwithstanding some attempts at codifying them, largely random observations on thematic and other types of coincidences among texts dominated by the use of fantasy.[1] But, as we will soon see, some works contemporary or almost contemporary with Todorov's share in at least some of its theoretical rigor. At any rate, the more satisfying analyses of the fantastic that have appeared since around 1970 orient themselves toward developing a theory capable of explaining in full its characteristics and the way that that genre, subgenre, or mode functions. This is, to a very large extent, the result of Todorov's systematic attempt to place an unquestionably loose notion within perfectly clear conceptual, structural, and chronological limits.

3

By defining the fantastic for the first time according to precise chronological and structural notions, Todorov brought to the forefront the conditions which make the existence of this genre (the fantastic is for him a full-fledged genre) possible, but which had until then remained virtually invisible. Consequently, his investigation of the fantastic effect in fiction has not only facilitated, but fostered the investigation of the essence of the fantastic. Almost all subsequent theoretical discussion of the fantastic appears, in fact, to fall within the parameters set by Todorov's monograph.

Todorov locates that essence, and the principle that characterizes the genre and serves to differentiate it from others, in the uncertainty and resulting hesitation felt by the reader about the nature of certain events narrated in the text which violate the laws of nature (did they, could they actually have occurred?). That hesitation is provoked by the way the text focuses on the supernatural while contrasting it with a realistic setting; it is very often expressed, in order to facilitate our experiencing it, by a character in the story. From this basic definition, Todorov proceeds to distinguish between the strange or uncanny and the marvelous, in their various literary embodiments, in relation to what he defines as the fantastic.

The uncanny and the marvelous use the fantastic—the appearance of the supernatural—differently and for different aims. When the uncertainty caused by it is resolved at the end by a more or less acceptable explanation, one which even if it is practically unbelievable pretends, nevertheless, to be based on natural, scientific laws, we are faced with the fantastic-uncanny.[2] This subgenre sustains "the hesitation characteristic of the true fantastic for a long period" (Todorov, *The Fantastic* 44). The fantastic-uncanny gradually dissolves toward the left of the spectrum devised by Todorov—uncanny / fantastic-uncanny / fantastic-marvelous / marvelous—as the strange, extraordinary, or incredible is more easily explained by the laws of reason, "into the general field of literature" (46). (Todorov adds that Dostoevsky's novels "may be included in the category of the uncanny" [ibid.].) For Todorov, the uncanny comprises also the horror story, which realizes only one of the conditions of the fantastic—the creation of fear at the appearance of the supernatural—but without, however, trying to cause uncertainty as to the actual possibility of the supernatural existing in the world of everyday reality. Actually, this brings the horror tale very close to Todorov's next category, the marvelous, inasmuch as the occurrence of the supernatural is fully accepted in it too. What excludes the horror story from the marvelous is that, contrary to what happens in the latter, the horror tale aims at (depends on) provoking a particular reaction: fear.

Like the uncanny, the marvelous unfolds into two categories. The fantastic-marvelous, "the class of narratives that are presented as fantastic and that end with an acceptance of the supernatural" (52), is closer, by definition, to the *pure fantastic* than is the fantastic-uncanny, since in the fantastic "the very fact that [the supernatural event] remains unexplained, unrationalized, suggests the actual existence of the supernatural" (ibid.). Like the fantastic-uncanny, the fantastic-marvelous sustains our uncertainty for some time. At the far right of Todorov's spectrum is the "pure marvelous," a category, like that of the uncanny, lacking "distinct frontiers" and encompassing "extremely diverse works [that] contain elements of the marvelous" (53). As with the pure uncanny or strange, in the pure marvelous the supernatural does not cause any hesitation in either characters or readers. In fact, it provokes "no particular reaction" as far as the question of the reality of the events narrated, since "it is not an attitude toward the events described which characterizes the marvelous, but the nature of those events" (54). In fairy tales, for example, the supernatural provokes no surprise at all; and the same happens normally in science fiction, thanks to the advancing of a purportedly rational explanation for the supernatural.

Only those works that succeed in generating in the reader a sustained uncertainty as to whether the not merely extraordinary, but virtually impossible events being narrated can be explained rationally, or are indeed supernatural, can be considered truly fantastic. What makes this hesitation possible is, in turn, the story's apparent adherence to the laws of the mimetic code, that is the faithful reproduction of reality. Such realism precludes the existence of the supernatural and assumes that there is a scientific explanation for all phenomena. The fantastic effect lasts only as long as does the reader's (and the character's) doubt vis-à-vis the nature of events which are in most cases eventually accepted or explained at the end of the narrative. At this point the fantastic effect ceases to exist, because the fantastic is, after all, a transitory, perpetually evanescent state existing not for all, but for only part of the duration of the reading of a text. "At the story's end, the reader makes a decision even if the character does not: he opts for one solution or the other, and thereby emerges from the fantastic. If he decides that the laws of reality remain intact and permit an explanation of the phenomena described, we say that the work belongs to another genre: the uncanny. If, on the contrary, he decides that new laws of nature must be entertained to account for the phenomena, we enter the genre of the marvelous" (41).

Todorov's conclusion regarding the nature of the fantastic depends on the absolute exclusion of both poetic and allegorical readings as the obvious ways of explaining the intention of the texts that he classifies as belonging to this genre. The reader's doubt is provoked only if the story pretends to be, and is understood by the reader as being realistic, except, of course, for that element which appears to be supernatural. In other words, the reader has to question the nature of the events and not, instead, "that of the very text which describes them" (58). The latter is precisely what happens in allegorical texts, which constantly point beyond what is being recounted, apparently following realistic conventions, and suggest that the text contains a half-hidden meaning for which the entire narrative is but a vehicle. (Realism in the strict sense shuns any type of teleological interpretation.) Thus, in an allegorical short story or novel, the supernatural occurs not in order to make us question our faith in reality, but as the vehicle for carrying the meaning of the story.

Poetry, or more appropriately modern lyrical poetry—since other forms of non-subjective poetry are still occasionally practiced—is by definition non-mimetic in relation to the outside world. The fantastic, on the other hand, requires "a reaction to events as they occur in the world evoked" (60). Consequently, the natural medium of the fantastic is the mimetic literary art par excellence, fiction. (Todorov's principles could, in theory, be applied to realistic theater, except that this medium does not lend itself easily to the inclusion of the uncanny and the marvelous, between which lives the fantastic.)

For Todorov, then, the fantastic, contrary to the marvelous and the strange, which have always been used in literature, developed as a genre in very close connection with the rise of realism, from the second half of the eighteenth century, through romanticism and naturalism, until the advent of modernism. The fantastic depends for its very existence on the existence of a reality which comes into question in relation to the possibility of certain events in the narrative. In many cases, the supernatural phenomenon is finally explained away as a mistake of perception on the part of the observer. But when it is fully accepted as a breach in nature's laws—and when the hesitation provoked by its appearance is not resolved by either fully accepting or rejecting the supernatural—its extraordinariness also supports, indirectly, the universal validity of those laws and, by extension, of mimetic literature. The fantastic, claims Todorov, served as a kind of "bad conscience" for a repressive era. Through it, the forbidden, and more specifically the sexually threatening found expression. In a philosophical way, the fantastic can be seen as an outlet for our immediate ancestors' doubts regarding the world's certainty at precisely the time when science was so intent on affirming it.

The collapse of scientism and the parallel absorption by fiction of the findings of psychoanalysis mark the beginning of the modern era. The latter phenomenon in particular facilitated the open portrayal of hidden feelings and desires; and the waning of positivism fostered a certain degree at least of distrust of physical reality. These two outlooks joined forces with the artist's increasing self-centeredness and interest in stylistic experimentation to decisively advance the main goal of the new artistic consciousness taking shape at the time: to liberate fiction from the need to copy reality. And thus, together with the demise of realism as the absolute norm for fiction, the fantastic, the genre that developed in the nineteenth century as a kind of secret critique of realism designed to plant a disturbing question inside the very world realist fiction was supposed to reproduce, also met its demise.

Todorov's study concludes with a discussion of Kafka's *The Metamorphosis* as the text that, all of a sudden, jumps out of the well-established parameters of the genre to which it appears to belong, the fantastic. In this novella no hesitation is ever evoked in the reader regarding the impossible transformation of the protagonist into an insect. As Todorov notes, both Gregor Samsa and his family, and especially the latter (Gregor thinks at first that he might simply be dreaming), do experience surprise at his sudden transformation into an insect, but never hesitate to accept as real this phenomenon which is introduced like any other fact, without particular emphasis and without focussing on it in a way that contrasts it with its realistic context.[3] Gregor has become a bug overnight, that's all; and what has happened is not explained rationally nor is its supernaturalness stressed in any way, as is the case in stories belonging to the fantastic-marvelous, which want their readers to dismiss their hesitation and accept the marvelous as a kind of new order. Once the protagonist's new nature is presented, Kafka goes on to describe in detail the human insect's physical movements as well as his emotions and thoughts, particularly as they relate to the various members of his family, whose psychological reactions are also fully described.

This basic realism works against the possibility of interpreting Samsa's metamorphosis allegorically. At no point in the course of the narrative does the author abandon his matter-of-fact approach to suggest an allegorical reading. If the reader wishes to pursue that avenue for the interpretation of the thoroughly impossible—and thus fantastic—central, or rather, initiating event of the novella, he will have to do so entirely on his own, contrary to what is customary in allegorical texts, including some of Kafka's own short parables, which include very definite suggestions for interpreting them. There is not, however, any other path to follow but the allegorical one for the curious reader who wishes to explore the meaning of *The Metamorphosis* as well as of its author's unfinished novels. We know as we read of Samsa's sudden transformation and K's mysterious trial, vain attempts to reach the castle's authorities, or peregrinations in the New World (the latter under a different name), that Kafka is saying something about guilt, evil, modern capitalism, the disappearance of God, bureaucracies, the contemporary world. At the same time, he alludes to so many of the conditions of our existence that the allegorical meaning multiplies itself and points in various, sometimes opposing directions at every turn of the narrative's course.

Such multiplying of allegorical meanings is, of course, alien to traditional allegory, since this would work against its goal of driving home its point as effectively and, in the long run, as clearly as possible. But what most markedly separates Kafka's technique from that characteristic of allegorical literature is the enormous distance between the hidden meaning of the text and the straight, realistic manner of narrating the most impossible of occurrences.

Todorov's analysis of the fantastic may be open to criticism for positing too strict a separation between Kafka's superbly original approach to the genre and the whole literature of the fantastic. The fantastic-marvel-ous, for example, also asks us to accept the supernatural, albeit not as part of our daily routine, as in Kafka's narratives.[4] While these narratives un-doubtedly constitute a major renovation of the genre to which they partially belong, they fall, broadly speaking, within the boundaries of allegorical literature despite the practical impossibility of determining their meaning. This fact points to the contiguity of the fantastic—considered now less as a genre (that is, a specific literary discourse that developed within rather precise historical boundaries) than as a general category or mode of fiction[5]—and allegory. As Todorov himself has noted, the fantastic shows a definite tendency toward allegory, a tendency, however, of which it can become aware only at the expense of suppressing its own most characteristic quality, the hesitation in front of the supernatural (*Poetics* 156).

Among those nineteenth-century representatives of the fantastic that he refers to in his analysis of the genre, Todorov identifies Henry James' *The Turn of the Screw* as ideally suited to illustrate the nucleus of his theory. In this novella the reader's uncertainty regarding the truth of the narrated events is never cleared either by a scientific explanation of them as being hallucinations suffered by the protagonist-narrator, or by their being declared to be indeed supernatural. Our uncertainty about the reality of the apparitions is maintained through the end of the narrative and remains even after we have closed the text. This effect is achieved mainly thanks to the perfect handling by James of the first-person narrator's perspective, which frames our perspective as readers.

Todorov's interpretation of *The Turn of the Screw* has been criticized as being unfair to James' intentions.[6] The governess's manuscript is introduced by its owner, someone who had known and admired her, and who then proceeds to read it aloud to a gathering of country-house guests who have been hearing ghost stories. While it is true that the manuscript's owner does not in any way question the truthfulness of his friend's account, what is said about her character (her youth and her infatuation with her employer, who orders her not ever to disturb him about her charges) and what she herself reveals in the course of recounting those bizarre experiences (she has an argument with the housekeeper regarding the girl; she insists at the end that Miles see the ghost, when in fact the boy does not see anything) is enough to cast some doubt on the soundness of her mind and the purity of her motives. Is she mad; is she omitting some crucial facts; did she make up the whole story in order to attract the children's guardian's attention? In other words, it may be that, in spite of the claims made by the governess as to the reality of the ghosts (which the narrative appears to accept as true), the author is all along leaving enough hints for us to reject her version and, consequently, also our hesitation regarding the existence of the supernatural.[7]

As Todorov notes, in *The Turn of the Screw* "perception [of what the protagonist is telling us] constitutes a screen" in relation to the "real" nature of "what is perceived" (105). This means that although in the end the supernatural is implicitly accepted as having occurred, due to the narrative's apparent reliance on the protagonist's account of her experiences, the rational explanation (the governess is a hysteric who hallucinates) which is suggested parallel to the supernatural one can then be developed by the reader in his own mind as the real conclusion of *The Turn of the Screw*. This is underscored by the fact that the story ends with the end of her account instead of going back to the frame within which it was told, a procedure that could have thrown some doubts on the veracity of the governess' testimony through appropriate comments by the listeners.

The ambiguity that characterizes James' novella represents the maximum possible effect achievable by the fantastic. Whether we give more weight to what points to the untruthfulness of the narrator, or prefer to rely on the forcefulness of her account (as does Todorov, indirectly, by concluding that the matter remains unresolved), is a decision deliberately left to the reader by an author who prefers not to voice any opinion of his own, not even through a character in the story. Although it is likely, as shown by his hints about her motives and personality, that James wanted us to assume the falseness of his protagonist's account (a conclusion supported by his total oeuvre, which is, basically, that of a realist who relies very strongly on psychological analysis),[8] he does not take anything away from the effect that the uncanny and possibly supernatural events recounted with so much detail and internal coherence have on us: that is, our uncertainty regarding whether such things can indeed happen.

That hesitation is exclusively a condition created by the text. Under no circumstances should we suppose that it is shared by the author beyond the intentions that govern the narrative, even when it is the authorial voice itself, instead of that of one of the characters, that questions reality through its reaction to the narrated events. Todorov's study of that masterful, perfect illustration of the genre, *The Turn of the Screw*, suggests that only very rarely do the authors of fantastic stories, no matter how strongly they may insist upon the reality of the impossible, actually leave the solid domain of the real and join their readers in doubting the impossibility of the supernatural. There are many instances, on the other hand, in which we are told in more or less straightforward ways to accept the supernatural as having taken place (the fantastic-marvelous, the marvelous).

Todorov calls the fantastic an evanescent genre, since it is defined by and depends on a hesitation that is usually temporary. But also ready to evaporate are the boundaries that the critic has so precisely defined between the provinces of the fantastic. Those evanescent borders depend on whether the fictional event or series of events is assumed to be somewhat explainable by the laws of reality (the *étrange pure* or uncanny), is explained rationally, although most of the time unconvincingly (the *fantastique-étrange*), or is accepted as being fully supernatural (the *fantastique-merveilleux*). The distinctions among the various levels of acceptance of either the falseness or the truth of uncanny, non-natural happenings tend in fact to blend with each other in the mind of the reader as nuances of one basic state created by the text: our initial surprise and subsequent uncertainty as to the nature (possible? impossible?) of what we are told took place. It is only through the critical act that we are able to differentiate among those various possibilities. Thus, Todorov's most important contribution to the study of the fantastic from a theoretical point of view is precisely the close study of those distinctions so that the genre can be analyzed according to a system.

Todorov's theory of the fantastic was the first among the many interpretations of the genre to establish a clear distinction between the fantastic proper (which he divided into the three more or less clearly separable categories of the uncanny, the fantastic-uncanny, and the fantastic-marvelous) and the pure marvelous (the fairy tale, for example), which, by suspending the laws of nature, assumes the supernatural, and does not rely for its effect on creating any kind of hesitation in the reader. This is so because those works very often want to lead the reader into translating the supernatural events or, as with science fiction (the "instrumental marvelous" for Todorov), the fantastic environment, into another context through the process known as allegory. In *The Metamorphosis*, Todorov's other limit example of the fantastic, the intention underneath the avoidance of doubt is also allegorical.

The fantastic, on the other hand, depends for its effect on the reader's initial—i.e., prior to the hesitation created by the narrative—rejection of the supernatural. That rejection results from the opposition between the real and the unreal, which constitutes the basis from which those texts operate in order to carry out their aims. For that opposition to be successful, the story must be told in a realistic manner, particularly with regard to the laws of psychological realism which had been adopted already by the eighteenth-century novel and which romanticism also accepted. Otherwise the introduction of the impossible element into the story would not have its desired effect of making us, however briefly, doubt reality. It should be noted, however, that although for all fantastic narratives, as defined by Todorov, reality and the laws of nature are a given, not all of them tell their story in as realistic a manner as does *The Turn of the Screw*. Many distort or evade reality in the pursuit of the fantastic effect, a function, in turn, of their having to press upon the reader the acceptance of the uncanny or the supernatural.

The centrality of doubt as the basis for the understanding of the fantastic cannot be stressed enough, even if, as we will see later, some narratives do not actually rely on it for their effect. Although the majority of readers do not believe that the laws of nature can be subverted, they enter, in the successful fantastic story, into a game with its author devised by the latter to make us suspend momentarily that belief in the impossibility of the supernatural to which we all so firmly subscribe in real life; to hesitate, in other words, between rejecting and accepting the possibility of the impossible. In the case of some exceptional texts, that uncertainty will transform itself into a doubt—a feeling more encompassing and of more lasting effects than the hesitation—that accompanies us after the

narrative has ended. There "are certain texts which sustain their ambiguity to the very end, i.e., even beyond the narrative itself" (Todorov, *The Fantastic* 43). Obviously, the key to the creation of those effects is the forceful introduction by the story of a supernatural event, something that denies the laws of nature as we know them.

In classical manifestations of the fantastic genre throughout the nineteenth century, the brief opposition of the real and the unreal was resolved in favor of one or the other within the narrative. Modernism, with its characteristic distrust of man's perception of reality, favors the indefinite suspension of the resolution of that opposition. The natural corollary of eliminating the conflict between the real and the unreal is the disappearance of the hesitation that their conflict had caused. James, in *The Turn of the Screw* treats the uncertainty in such a way that it outlasts the closing of the narrative (while in fact it was unfounded from the start). He accomplishes this through the importance he gives to his unreliable narrator, who insists on saying, and in fact makes us believe that she is being besieged by ghosts. While he achieved the most perfect fantastic story possible by thus prolonging the duration of the hesitation that defines the genre, James also, by stretching to its limit the tension between the real and the unreal on which the genre's existence—its effect—depends, contributed to the demise of the classical fantastic. The next step is the disappearance, together with that of the conflict between the real and the unreal, of all uncertainty, as we saw happen in Kafka's fictions. This is also characteristic of later manifestations of the fantastic.

It should be stressed that what Todorov calls the fantastic genre is, as Jonathan Culler explains, but a particular use of fantasy: that in which "the reader helping to construct the laws of an imaginative universe is forced to hesitate between two kinds of law" ("Literary Fantasy"). That suspension of interpretation "produces a self-conscious consideration of the way in which one goes about understanding a fictional world," since each of the alternative worlds presented to the consideration of the reader "has different interpretative consequences" (33). As with the other two roles that fantasy plays in literature—a "premise" in "metaphorical" literature (that which postulates a world different from but analogous to our own) and a "deviation from an order" in "metonymical" literature (which presents a world that is a previously unencountered portion of our own [32])—its effect in the fantastic is based "on our basic assumption that literature is always mimetic and will refer us to a world of some kind" (33). This assumption does not apply at all, of course, to works such as surrealist poems (for some critics surrealism represents the most

subversive and liberating use of fantasy), "where the process of constructing imaginative worlds is parodied, blocked, and hedged about with so
many uncertainties that it comes to seem irrelevant" (ibid.).

My analysis of Borges' and Cortázar's "fantastic" stories will use
as its basis the notions of the appearance of an impossible element within
an otherwise realistic setting, and of the uncertainty that this provokes.
While I rely for the definition of these notions on Todorov, my own approach will pay due attention to their modification in the practice of the
writers studied, a modification which reflects the transformation of the
fantastic as it moved away from its origin.

In her book on the fantastic, *Le récit Fantastique*, Irene Bessière
criticizes Todorov's *Introduction*, whose arguments she finds inexact and
farfetched. Yet she comes to very much the same conclusion as the target
of her criticism with respect to the central function for fantastic narratives
of our hesitation (which she calls *incertitude*) regarding the pretended
reality of events that seem supernatural. Bessière sets for the genre the
same chronological limits that Todorov described. It begins, she explains,
with Cazotte toward the end of the eighteenth century, and lasts as long
as does realism, the reason being that both realism and the fantastic are
linked to the progressive weakening of religious beliefs. This weakening
enables literature to introduce the supernatural within totally secular
contexts, and give it the same standing as the reality it attempts to deny,
circumvent, or question. Bessière also concurs with Todorov on the
necessity for the fantastic to be firmly rooted in reality if it is to depict
the impossible convincingly; otherwise we would not hesitate before its
presence or be tempted to accept it. Though it may assume a dreamlike
tone for all or part of the narrative, a fantastic story has to proceed within
the framework appropriate to realistic description; it cannot, at least
openly, move into the realm of allegory.

These conclusions, which follow Bessière's remarks on how the
genre grew out of the secularization of literature, confirm and strengthen
Todorov's arguments. (Bessière quotes Foucault on how, with the triumph
of the Enlightenment the *déraison* was silenced out of accepted literary
discourse and forced to express itself through the fantastic. This is, of
course, an interpretation of a historical process very close to Todorov's
own.) Bessière, however, ends up discussing not the fantastic, but fantasy.
This much broader category aims, in Bessière's view, at exposing the
arbitrariness of the dominant cultural order, which it wishes to deconstruct
in order to replace it with the uncertain, and thus show the limits of reason
and the way unreality coexists with—in fact, within—reality.

This provocative interpretation of the fantastic as the literary expression of fantasy is philosophical in nature. As such it is not bound by the limits of a particular genre the way Todorov's study is, and it does not attempt to analyze the "fantastic" effect on the reader. Bessière's thesis is "semantic" rather than "syntactic" or formalistic, and indeed she offers in her book rich discussions of the possibilities of fantasy for literature in general, and of the cultural role of the fantastic.[9] Since its focus is on the possibilities offered by fantasy as a weapon for questioning reality, this study does not help very much toward the systematic investigation of fantastic texts, whether from the genre's classical or contemporary period. It does feature, however, lucid discussions of some individual fantastic works as well as illuminating comments on the fantastic vis-à-vis the social world. In the long run, the subject of Bessière's book is modernist and post-modernist literature, which she sees as being particularly conscious of the intrinsic irreality of all literary texts and of artistic artifacts in general (thus she feels justified in studying, in a book which is purportedly about the fantastic, Cortázar's novel *Hopscotch*, since it deals in depth with the function of the imagination, art, and literature).

Christine Brooke-Rose ("Historical Genres") criticizes Todorov for relying wholly on the historical parameters of the fantastic—which he does in order to establish the conditions for defining it as a genre—rather than developing the theoretical possibilities suggested by his study. Todorov succeeds in defining a set of requirements for the fantastic in literature; but he does so only by inferring them from what was achieved by a certain group of texts, thus failing to allow for all possible developments within the genre. This is demonstrated for Brooke-Rose by Todorov's treatment of Kafka, whose stories, because they do not make use of the characteristic hesitation, he prefers to situate outside of his genre.

Brooke-Rose argues that the pure fantastic is a permanently vanishing element which can exist only in a portion of a text. Todorov had also defined as evanescent the condition that makes a text fantastic, since that condition lasts only as long as our hesitation. He remarked also that, if we did not treat literary texts as unities which should not be broken up, but were instead willing to examine certain parts of certain texts in isolation, and temporarily omit their ending (when the strange events are explained and the hesitation is resolved), those texts would become part of the fantastic (Todorov, *The Fantastic* 43). He also states, however, that given the fact that a few texts are capable of sustaining the doubt to the very end of a narrative and even beyond it, "it would be wrong to conclude that the fantastic can exist *only* [my italics] in a part of a work" (ibid.). Brooke-Rose, on the other hand, suggests stretching the uncanny beyond the line that separates the fantastic-uncanny from the marvelous, to include within the fantastic slightly strange but basically realistic novels (such as Vonnegut's), which in her view represent the coming together of the uncanny and the marvelous.[10]

All of this leads to questioning one of Todorov's basic points: the rejection of allegory as a carrier for the fantastic, on the grounds that it excludes, by definition, the hesitation with which the fantastic is identified, shifting the focus away from the reality that the narrative is supposed to portray—interwoven with supernatural events—to the external meaning for which it is a vehicle. Brooke-Rose distinguishes between "an allegory we may find encoded in the text" (what Todorov calls "allegory" in the course of his discussion of the fantastic)[11] and "a *subjective* [my italics] allegorical reading, such as anyone can make of any text" (*Rhetoric* 154), including modern and contemporary ones, which we assume to be nonfigural just as we assume medieval works to be figural. This leads to "the (fictional) 'truth' of the story [becoming] the 'literal' level in allegory ('literal' here in its older sense of the story as opposed to its allegorical meaning)" (ibid.). Proceeding along this line, Brooke-Rose proposes a "fantastic" reading of Dante's *Commedia* (was the poet's journey a mere dream, or was it a supernatural event?), comparable to the two levels of meaning generated by the reader's hesitation regarding the events narrated in *The Turn of the Screw* (was it an hallucination, or did ghosts actually appear?). And recognizing that in the "pure fantastic" there is no hierarchical relationship between those (basically) two possibilities—in fact they are mutually exclusive—Brooke-Rose argues that a similar paradoxical element is very much part of medieval allegory in its more sophisticated manifestations. In Langland's *The Vision Concerning Piers Plowman*, for instance, the elements of the *sensus allegoricus* (the laity, the clergy, the episcopacy) can be equated with those of the *sensus anagogicus* (God the Father, the Son, and the Holy Ghost) only "on a purely abstract level" (*Rhetoric* 155), as happens also in the *Divine Comedy*.

Brooke-Rose concludes that the fantastic "as defined by Todorov" is but a "modern development (nonhierarchized levels, a stronger paradox) of medieval allegory, two among various ways of writing metaphorically, or on several levels, or paradigmatically" (156). On the other hand, the marvelous, including science fiction, tends toward "encoded allegory," just as the uncanny "can easily tend toward at least a moral meaning."[12] The ambiguity characteristic of the fantastic could also be interpreted as prefiguring the way many modern non-fantastic texts "can be read on several and often paradoxically contradictory levels'' (ibid.). In the final account, she suggests, the "evanescent element" that "defines the pure genre'' is "merely a particular (historical) manifestation of a more general feature (at least two contradictory readings) which can and perhaps should be found in all sophisticated (complex) narratives'' (ibid.).

Todorov's pure fantastic, instead of being limited to a historical genre, becomes, in this view, emblematic of the possibility of reading any text on two levels, the literal and the metaphorical (a category which includes allegory), both always present in it, but often also mutually exclusive. In other words, our hesitation regarding the events narrated in *The Turn of the Screw* or in *La Venus d'Ille* is indicative of, on the one hand, the plurality of interpretations found in so many modern texts, and on the other, the complexity of the best medieval allegory. The former direction looks toward the present, the latter toward the past. One would have, however, to eliminate from this equation between modern plurality of meaning and medieval double meaning, the more realistic texts belonging to the period when the fantastic genre emerged. Those texts preclude, in general, the possibility of more than one interpretation, including the allegorical. And even in those texts that do include several levels of allegory or various possible interpretations of events situated between the semantic and syntactic components of the text, hesitation is not a significant factor, according to the model proposed by Brooke-Rose. With those qualifications, Brooke-Rose's comments remain extremely useful, especially for the consideration of the role of allegory in the modern fantastic.

While Bessière's aim was to discuss the role and possibilities of the literary expression of the human imagination, or fantasy, Brooke-Rose seems preoccupied primarily with the problematization of reality characteristic of modern fiction. For a paradigm of this she proposes the genre described by Todorov, thus deliberately de-historicizing it in order to make better use of its theoretical possibilities.[13] She calls attention to the great complexity of the pure fantastic by comparison with the uncanny and the marvelous as well as with realistic texts (which are complex in other, ideological and thematic ways). In texts belonging to those categories of literary discourse the *fabula* is transparent; in the fantastic, on the other hand, we have always two *fabulae*, both apparently simple and clear, but actually not so, since they are mutually exclusive. It is because the discourse of the fantastic is so baffling that its texts tend to be short: it would be impossible to sustain that tension between opposing stories for very long (*Rhetoric* 229).

Eric Rabkin, in *The Fantastic in Literature* also criticizes Todorov's approach as too narrow, proposing instead to see the fantastic as a basic mode of human knowledge. His conclusions, although somewhat more limited in their scope and theoretical possibilities than Bessière's and Brooke-Rose's (a function of the book's focus: fantastic fiction in the nineteenth and twentieth centuries, with some incursions into the visual arts), parallel nevertheless their view of the fantastic as a permanent feature of fiction writing. Rabkin recognizes that fantasy (which he is careful to distinguish from literature of escape) is a much larger category than the fantastic, but he ends up dealing primarily with the former, which is perhaps unavoidable given his approach. Rabkin refuses to limit the fantastic to the specific characteristics of one genre, arguing that "fantasies" belong to several genres—including the fantastic—which vary considerably among themselves.

Although he accepts the importance of the hesitation for defining the fantastic ("an acute and useful insight" on the part of Todorov [118 n]), Rabkin would like to capitalize on it by modifying its role and also by locating it in aspects of narrative other than the plot, so that it could function not in relation to the external norms imposed by reality through the doubts of a character with whom we identify, but rather to microcontextual variations within the text (this refers to the relationship between the "fantastic" event and the text within which it occurs). Once we agree that the hesitation does not depend on the plot and how it develops, Rabkin claims, its study could lead to larger narratological studies. At the same time, he argues that all art is fantasy, because art offers a safe and controlled world where we can suspend disbelief.

This approach reflects, as do all those that focus on fantasy rather than on its application to a specific fantastic genre, the etymology of the word fantastic, which is of course the same as that of fantasy. For Aristotle that word meant the capacity to reproduce sensorial data without the objects that provoked them in the first place. It thus became synonymous with imagination. Since Rabkin is not dealing with a specific genre (neither are Bessière and Brooke-Rose, except that the latter keeps her discussion within the boundaries of Todorov's definition of the fantastic in order to explore the theoretical possibilities included in it), he will talk about how much more "fantastic" this or the other text is depending on whether the events narrated are more or less "fantastic"—i.e., impossible—in relation to the actual world. He does so especially in regard to science fiction, a genre which for Todorov falls outside the fantastic since it does not aim at provoking our hesitation.

W. I. Irwin's study of the fantastic, *The Game of the Impossible: A Rhetoric of Fantasy*, appears to be closer to Todorov's, inasmuch as he wishes to deal with the fantastic's rhetoric, or how it is that "fantasies"—Todorov's *littérature fantastique*—handle the overt violation of what is generally accepted as possible, and seemingly manage to transform into fact what is actually contrary to fact. The connotations of fantasy for Irwin are very different from those it has for Rabkin, mainly because in differentiating between fantasy and the fantastic, Irwin characterizes the latter as what for Rabkin and others is fantasy, i.e., not a literary genre, but an activity which engages the imagination. "Fantasy," on the other hand, demands the use of our intellect. It is a mistake for Irwin merely to equate "fantasy" with the untrue, the implausible, the thoroughly exotic. What for this critic defines the genre, is our *knowing* that we are dealing with a contravention of reality within a sort of "game" in which the anti-real plays against the real. Because he focuses on the concept of the game between author and reader rather than on the former's ability to engage the latter's belief in his portrayal of the impossible as true, Irwin dismisses the role of the hesitation in "fantasies." The writer of fantasies, he claims, avoids causing the uncertainty that Todorov took to be essential; on the contrary, everything in a successful fantasy, according to Irwin, should be clear and certain.[14]

Tobin Siebers in *The Romantic Fantastic* sees the fantastic as a product of the romantic imagination, which stressed difference and rebellion. The fantastic highlights difference by portraying that which is absent, that which goes beyond the human. The supernatural, then, is intrinsic to the fantastic, understood as the literature through which the power of superstitious beliefs is expressed. Siebers's discussion of the fantastic is limited by his identification of it with superstition, which in his view, the fantastic makes manifest. It is further limited by its concentration on the romantic fantastic. Notice, however, that linking the fantastic with superstition is not far from linking it with the unconscious, as Todorov did. Siebers recognizes the importance of the hesitation as the principle that identifies a fantastic narrative, albeit interpreting it as an expression of our superstitious nature.

A very useful review of fantastic literature is Rosemary Jackson's *Fantasy: The Literature of Subversion*. As in the cases of Bessière and Rabkin, this critic focuses on fantasy, which she defines by associating it with imagination and desire. Literary fantasies are free from the conventions and restraints of more realistic texts precisely because they aim at transcending reality and escaping the human condition. They do this by violating that which is normally accepted or by constructing, through the inversion of elements of our world, alternative worlds.

Jackson is particularly concerned with exploring the relationship between fantasy and desire (the former unveils or expels—in those cases when it is a disturbing presence—the latter), and fantasy and the unsaid or unseen (this takes us to the roots of fantasy in the ancient myths). She recognizes the importance of Todorov's treatise and agrees in general with his matter-of-fact approach. She calls him to task, at the same time, for not paying the attention it deserves to the historical and cultural framework for the development of the fantastic genre, and for forgetting the social and political implications of the texts he studies. Jackson also criticizes Todorov's repudiation of psychoanalytical theory as irrelevant to the study of a literature that actually deals with the unconscious.[15]

Since she is discussing fantasy rather than the fantastic, Jackson sees her subject ("literary fantasies") as a *mode* which is not bound by the conventions of any given age and from which "a number of related genres emerge" (7), such as "romance literature or 'the marvelous' (including fairy tales and science fiction), 'fantastic literature' (including stories by Poe, Isak Dinesen, Maupassant, Gautier, Kafka, H. Lovecraft) and related tales of abnormal psychic states, delusion, hallucination, etc." (ibid.).

Like Todorov, Jackson focuses on the question of how literary fantasies produce their effect on readers. This is accomplished, she proposes, by the lack of a satisfactory internal explanation for a phenomenon which violates the laws of nature by which the action of the narrative seems, nevertheless, to abide. The result of that contradiction is, of course, our hesitation. Like Todorov again, Jackson insists on distinguishing sharply between allegory and poetry on the one hand, and fantasy on the other. Fantasy resists the conceptualization characteristic of the first and the metaphorical structure of the second. Jackson concludes that the fantastic, because it is located uneasily between the realistic and the marvelous, has a subversive function within our culture.[16]

All of these interpretations of the fantastic aim, by defining or redefining their subject, at expanding its range beyond that of a specific historical genre developed in the nineteenth century, whose life coincides, roughly, with that of the realistic novel. Some of them are extremely useful in the interpretation of particular texts that are generally characterized as being "fantastic" (regardless of whether they are considered to belong to a genre, as Todorov would have it, or to a larger category of fiction having to do with the use of fantasy); but those interpretations do not help much in the task of explaining how the fantastic works, or in studying the forms it takes. By extending the concept of the fantastic to coincide with that of imagination, they actually call for a return to precisely that state in the interpretation of narratives dealing with the supernatural into which Todorov wanted to introduce some rigorous notions that would help us move beyond general assumptions and vague definitions. His identification of the fantastic effect with the reader's hesitation at the irruption of the supernatural within a realistic context, and of the fantastic genre, by extension, with the intention of producing that doubt (an intention not typical of the normal use of fantasy in literature) helps more than any other analysis of the principles governing those texts toward clarifying their structure and goals. Defined as a basic operation of the human mind, fantasy is just too broad a concept (Rabkin deals in his book with *Alice in Wonderland*, Robbe-Grillet's novels, Borges' *ficciones*, and science fiction). Depicting the ambiguity intrinsic to reality appears, on the other hand, to be but the natural aim of the increasingly sophisticated interaction between reader and text that the post-modern writer favors and even deliberately seeks.[17]

A convincing (and far-reaching in its implications) critique of Todorov's interpretation of the fantastic is implied in Hélène Cixous' discussion of Freud's explanation of the uncanny or *unheimlich* ("La fiction et ses fantômes"). He defines the uncanny as that which, because it is unknown and apparently supernatural, appears as terrifying, sinister, ghastly, yet which points to something long-known and familiar (thus having the quality of being *heimlich*), that has undergone a process of repression due to its threatening nature (as with the fear of castration in children).[18]

Cixous argues that an interpretation of fantastic texts that tries to confine the fantastic within the boundaries of rationality, by connecting the fantastic effect with psychic processes that do not appear as such in the text, results in impoverishing those works. To remove the uncertainty from them is to take away a good deal of their complexity. Who is to tell us, asks Cixous, that the fear of castration, which Freud sees as being the final explanation of Hoffmann's "Sandman" story, does not lead to even deeper secrets? This is why she objects to Freud's attempt to explain scientifically the uncertainty generated by the fantastic. For her the effect of fiction depends precisely on that doubt, on that which resists analysis and never disappears completely, perhaps because it points to the passage between the living and the dead. Cixous agrees with Freud's definition of the *unheimlich* as the familiar hidden, as well as with his interpretation of the role of our doubt vis-à-vis it (and in regard to the doubt, Freud's analysis comes close to Todorov's). But she adds that the *unheimlich* is a highly complex effect which filters into us through the smallest of openings and can lead to many visions and interpretations (the doll Olympia in Hoffmann's story could represent, for instance, death slowly moving toward life).[19]

This is a forceful and coherent statement of the value of fantasy in literature and the need to let ourselves be drawn into the ambiguities that the text plays with. Cixous calls, basically, for the same thing that Bessière and Rabkin do. Yet she avoids the sort of confusion that these critics create as they attempt to develop a method out of what is basically an anti-system argument by futilely subdividing the very broad categories that they had initially established, in order to make them applicable to the study of the actual texts of the fantastic.

As we move closer to the central purpose of this study, which is the examination of contemporary texts by Borges and Cortázar usually assumed to belong to the fantastic genre, it seems appropriate to review what the Argentinean critic, Ana María Barrenechea, who has also written some of the most illuminating pages on Borges,[20] has to say about the fantastic. In her "Ensayo de una tipología de la literatura fantástica," Barrenechea approaches the study of the fantastic by way of twentieth-century Spanish American literature, which is particularly rich in texts belonging to that genre. Her aim is to modify Todorov's theory to make apparent some characteristics of the fantastic that have, in her view, been neglected by Todorov.

Barrenechea sees the fantastic as derived from the existence, implicit or explicit, of abnormal, unnatural, or unreal phenomena alongside their opposites, which results in a problematization of the contrast presented by their coexistence. Notice that she says "problematization" rather than "hesitation," since for her the doubt about the nature of abnormal, supernatural, or unreal happenings plays no role in defining the fantastic. Barrenechea claims that the fantastic can exist also where there is no questioning of the strange, as in the "pure marvelous" and the "pure uncanny." Following a line of reasoning that brings her close to Brooke-Rose's thesis, Barrenechea remarks that poetic and allegorical readings of a text—which, for Todorov, work, by definition, against the fantastic effect—cannot automatically be excluded from the fantastic genre. Poetry is not by nature non-representational, as we tend to think of it nowadays; nor are contemporary allegories as easily explainable as classical ones; and thus both leave room for the use of the fantastic in its pure form.

The confrontation of the real and the unreal, in fact, facilitates crossing the barriers between those categories and mixing their respective characteristics. For Borges, says Barrenechea, there is no genre that cannot include the fantastic (but perhaps, by the same token, there is not for Borges a single genre that can be defined as fantastic); and actually, in Borges' view, allegory can reinforce the fantastic when it expresses the senselessness of the real world by making it appear unreal. Todorov's classification is thus incomplete because it leaves out that fiction which deals with what is natural and in which no doubt is generated regarding the reality of the events portrayed. There are, after all, Barrenechea goes on to say, other means, perhaps more subtle than the character/reader's hesitation, of provoking the same effect as that caused by witnessing the violation of the world's order, i.e., the "fantastic" effect. She concludes that there are three basic types of fantastic texts, depending on whether the contents of the narrative belong to the natural order, the non-natural order, or a mixture of both.

In her more recent "Literatura fantástica," Barrenechea restates some of the preceding arguments and also points out that the fantastic, regardless of whether it is a genre or not, certainly exists as a literary tradition as well as a commercial object produced by writers and marketed by publishers. She then explains the essential part that the data coming from sociocultural codes plays in the creation of fantastic literature. The mystic and the marvelous, for example, are not generally considered to belong to the fantastic because they fall too far outside what is accepted as reality according to the cultural code under whose premises we live. However, a fantastic text can take as its subject the beliefs of groups outside the culture of the author and absorb the abnormal event by inscribing in the text the appropriate cultural codes according to which the categories of normal and abnormal are elaborated by that culture. It may also simply include unusual events without offering any explanation of them.

This article focuses on García Márquez, a writer who is generally considered to be a "magical realist" (we will come back to this concept), and whose greatest originality consists in evenly distributing the traits that characterize natural and unnatural beings in such a fashion that the most unusual is accepted without any hesitation, but also without bringing it within the boundaries of ordinary literary conventions and cultural models—accepting, on the contrary, that it simply falls outside those norms. This points, in regard to the evolution of the fantastic, to a shift in the way that cultural codes are used. Where the codes informing early fantastic texts were clearly those of the social group which produced them, these have become increasingly ambiguous and heterodox in more recent texts such as those of García Márquez, and less and less "placeable," as the subversion of the mimetic tradition progresses and concern with verisimilitude decreases. What was previously presented in terms of "reality" being "violated" is now presented as a known code—that according to which verisimilitude is defined—into which an unknown (but no more or less viable) code intrudes.

Barrenechea's thoughts on the fantastic represent, in many ways, a sensible proposal for understanding it. She accepts—as do some of the other critics discussed above—the usefulness of a principle such as the hesitation, uncertainty, or problematization (her own term) to define the appearance of the fantastic. However, like most of those critics, she too objects to Todorov's theory, finding it too narrow in scope. Barrenechea wants to include within the fantastic some texts in which there is no problematization of reality at all; but she does not explain through what means such texts can provoke, as she claims, the same effect on the reader as do texts that cause us to hesitate between the real and the unreal. It is worth remembering here Todorov's assertion that the mere inclusion of the supernatural in a narrative, unless it is specifically directed at provoking our hesitation about the narrated events, is a useless tool for defining the fantastic, since it would lead to dumping together in the same category all those texts in which supernatural events take place, from the *Illiad* on.[21] As her ideas on the fantastic evolved, Barrenechea began to emphasize the role of socio-cultural codes in determining what is and what is not fantastic, an area of inquiry that has, in fact, been neglected by most critics. She also seems to have rejected her previous claim that the marvelous and related genres could be considered to belong to the fantastic.

Notes

1. This is how I would characterize books such as Caillois' *Au coeur du fantastique* (1965), Castex's *Le conte fantastique en France* (1951), Louis Vax's *L'art et la littérature fantastique* (1960), Penzoldt's *The Supernatural in Fiction* (1952), or Schneider's *La littérature fantastique en France* (1964). See the bibliography in Todorov's *Introduction*, 186–88.

2. After explaining that the fantastic occupies the duration of our uncertainty before a phenomenon that demands to be interpreted either as an illusion of the senses or as a real event, Todorov points out that his definition is not original. This is what the "Russian philosopher and mystic Vladimir Solovyov" said in the nineteenth century: "In the genuine fantastic, there is always the external and formal possibility of a simple explanation of phenomena, but at the same time this explanation is completely stripped of all internal probability." Todorov adds that "The possibility of a hesitation between the two [types of explanation, through natural or supernatural causes, of an uncanny phenomenon] creates the fantastic effect" (*The Fantastic*, 25–26). Rosemary Jackson, in *Fantasy: The Literature of Subversion*, says that Todorov "discovered the kernel of his theories in the writing of" Solovyov (27).

3. In his discussion of *The Metamorphosis* (*The Fantastic* 169–72, at 169), Todorov quotes Camus on Kafka: "We shall never be sufficiently amazed about this lack of amazement."

4. Todorov notes "that the best science fiction texts are organized analogously [to Kafka's, as *narratives* to be read on the literal level]. The initial data are supernatural: robots, extraterrestrial beings.... The narrative movement consists in obliging us to see how close these apparently marvelous elements are to us, to what degree they are present in our life" (*The Fantastic* 172).

5. By "mode" I mean something different from Robert Scholes' "ideal types" of narrative fiction, which are based, in turn, on how fiction renders the world: better, worse, or approximately equal to the way it actually is ("Towards a Poetics of Fiction: An Approach through Genre," *Novel* 2 [1969]: 101–11). Although the fantastic considered as a mode could fit, very broadly speaking, into Scholes' first category (the one corresponding to romance), it is more useful for our purposes to think of it as an approach to materials chosen in view of certain authorial goals. This is also how Rosemary Jackson discusses the fantastic as a mode ("The Fantastic As a Mode," in *Fantasy*, esp. 35). We will come back to this problem later.

6. See in this regard, "*The Turn of the Screw* and Its Critics: An Essay in Non-Methodology," in Brooke-Rose's *Rhetoric*.

7. Brooke-Rose characterizes *The Turn of the Screw* as its author's " 'intended' test of his reader's inattention, a text composed on the very principle of ambiguity." It is also "a text structured (intentionally or not) on the same principle that a neurosis is structured," i.e., it tries "to drag the 'other' down into itself, into the neurosis, the other being here the reader" (*Rhetoric* 156). See the definitive analysis of the James novella that follows (Parts 3, 7, and 8).

8. He wrote, however, many ghost stories. Todorov explains this in "The Ghosts of Henry James" (in *Poetics*) by pointing out that for James "Objects, 'things' do not exist (or if they exist, do not interest James); what intrigues him is the experience his characters can have of objects. There is no 'reality' except a psychic one; the material and physical fact is normally absent, and we never know anything about it except the way in which various persons can experience it . . . the only reality is imaginary, there are no facts but psychic ones. Truth is always a special case, someone's truth; consequently, to ask 'does this ghost really exist?' has no meaning the moment it exists for someone" (184–85).

9. See especially chapters 4 and 5 and the discussion of verisimilitude and the problematization of reality.

10. See *Rhetoric*, part 4. The book includes extremely illuminating discussions of metafiction and postmodern literature.

11. Todorov summarizes the definition of allegory this way: it "implies the existence of at least two meanings for the same words; according to some critics, the first meaning must disappear, while others require that the two be present together. Secondly, this double meaning is indicated in the work in an *explicit* fashion: it does not proceed from the reader's interpretation (whether arbitrary or not)" (*The Fantastic* 63).

12. Page 156. See in this regard Brooke-Rose's discussion of science fiction in *Rhetoric*, parts 2 and 4.

13. Brooke-Rose criticizes Todorov for not developing all the theoretical possibilities of the genre that he postulates, for actually relying on a historical genre ("Historical Genres" 150–54).

14. Irwin argues that in *The Metamorphosis* the reader believes that the transformation of the protagonist into an insect is a fact; otherwise he would experience an intellectual rejection precluding a constructive response. This is so because fantasies persuade the reader to accept the impossible, but without abandoning the convention that opposes it. Fairy tales, on the other hand, are anti-fantasies, since they appeal to a belief that although it is officially rejected, still retains credence. Science fiction, finally, deals with the amazing and highly improbable, but not

with the impossible.

15. This is for Jackson "one of the major shortcomings of Todorov's book": He insists that " 'Psychosis and neurosis are not the explication of the themes of fantastic literature' (154). Yet his attention to themes of self and other, of 'I' and 'not-I,' opens on to issues of interrelationship and of the determination of relations between human subjects by unconscious desire, issues which can only be understood by turning to psychoanalysis." She then cites Bellemin-Noël, who says "it is a mistake to suppose that the only use of psychoanalysis would be to account for the content of fantasy. On the contrary, the problem is one of examining 'how the *formal* aspects of the fantastic are themselves in liaison with the workings and/or the configurations of the *unconscious discourse*' (117)" (*Fantasy* 61–62).

16. In chapter 5, "Fantastic Realism," Jackson claims that fantasy was not an "alternative" literary form during the nineteenth century, but one on which mainstream novelists relied, so that often "within the main, realistic text, there exists another non-realistic one, camouflaged and concealed, but constantly present" (123–24). The book includes a discussion of many critics and practitioners of the fantastic and of various readings of it.

17. Other useful books on the fantastic are Jacques Finné's *La littérature fantastique: Essai sur l'organisation surnaturelle* (Bruxelles: Université de Bruxelles, 1980); Harry Belevan's *Teoría de lo fántástico* (Barcelona: Anagrama, 1976); C. N. Manlove's *Modern Fantasy: Five Studies* (Cambridge: Cambridge Univ. Press, 1975); Max Milner's *La fantasmagorie: Essai sur l'optique fantastique* (Paris: PUF, 1982); and Kathryn Hume's *Fantasy and Mimesis* (New York and London: Methuen, 1984).

18. In his 1919 essay "The Uncanny" (*The Standard Edition of the Psychological Works*, ed. James Strachey, 24 vols. [London, 1953], 17:217–52), Freud notes that the appearance of the uncanny causes intellectual uncertainty, doubt. He states that not everything that provokes a feeling of uncanniness is connected with repressed desires, and advances that there are examples of the uncanny, taken from literature, that contradict his hypothesis. Freud distinguishes between the experience of the uncanny in real life and in literature (the first is conditioned much more simply and is limited to fewer occasions; the uncanny in literature is not submitted to the same type of reality testing, since the storyteller, who has at his disposal more means of creating the uncanny, chooses whether the world he creates is going to coincide or not with the real one, and we as readers accept his rules). The uncanny is not present in fairy tales or in other literary settings which admit the supernatural without creating in us a conflict of judgement. To generate the uncanny, a writer takes

advantage of our naturally superstitious nature; for that feeling to be effective, we should be kept in the dark as long as possible. Freud adds that the uncanny in literature is directly dependent on the realism of the setting.

19. Cixous points out that it is impossible to translate *unheimlich* into French. This is so, in her opinion, because of the characteristic logocentrism of French culture and its reliance on a rational interpretation of reality. She adds that there is no fantastic literature in France except through "infiltration" from Germany ("La fiction et ses fantômes" 37-38).

20. See her *La expresión de la irrealidad en la obra de Jorge Luis Borges* (México: Fondo de Cultura Económica, 1957).

21. "We cannot conceive a genre which would regroup all works in which the supernatural intervenes and which would thereby have to accomodate Homer as well as Shakespeare, Cervantes as well as Goethe. The supernatural does not characterize works closely enough, its extension is much too great" (*The Fantastic* 34).

Chapter Two

Borges and the Fantastic

We will begin the study of Borges' contribution to fantastic literature by looking at some of his own theoretical statements related to the fantastic. Those with the widest implications occur in the essay "Narrative Art and Magic," of 1932 (in *Discussion* 71–79), three years prior to the publication of his first book of stories, *Universal History of Infamy*. In this essay, while discussing a novel in verse by William Morris on the adventures of Jason (*The Life and Death of Jason*, 1867) along with Poe's *Gordon Pym*, Borges asks himself how it is that both texts manage to capture their readers' interest through the "spontaneous suspension of disbelief that is, for Coleridge, poetic faith" (72; my translation). He concludes that this is a result of their sustaining an appearance of verisimilitude. This is, of course, the same quality that, in Todorov's theory, makes our hesitation possible. Yet neither one of the texts that Borges deals with here aims at producing the fantastic effect, and both actually fall outside the realist tradition.

Borges' arguments in this essay are in fact difficult to follow, to some extent because the categories that he employs (the novel's devices, suspension of disbelief, persuasion, causality, anthropology's law of sympathy) lack sufficient critical definition. In addition, Borges was at the time still writing in a highly synthetic and elusive style of avant-garde—and more specifically ultraísta[1]—origin. The conclusion of the essay is, at any rate, an indirect rejection of causality as being appropriate only to the "slow novel of characters," and not to the adventure story ("the novel

29

of uninterrupted vicissitudes" [77]). The latter, rather than feigning a concatenation of motives that pretends to reproduce those of the real world, chooses the "lucid and atavic" (ibid.) order provided by magic. Borges considers this type of novel to be above any other in artistic quality. However, if the texts under discussion are not, as he suggests, governed by a causality of a realistic type, then their success as narratives should also have nothing to do (as he had initially proposed) with our acceptance of their impossibility on the basis of a subtle gradation of effects devised to make them appear *vraisemblable*. It could be, nevertheless, that by the text's "success" Borges simply means its acceptance by a relatively large reading public. This is what his equating literature with films, also of the adventure type, suggests (he explains the popularity of the latter as a result of their ignoring causality).

Borges concludes that instead of being governed by a psychological causality, these works, literary as well as cinematographic, are governed by the causality characteristic of magic. This is based, in turn, on the law of sympathy between objects,[2] which creates a new and higher type of causality, more potent because it is ancestral and mysterious. Borges states that the "dangerous harmony" (78) of magic (*magia simpática*) also governs the novel, citing in support of this thesis three stories by Chesterton, the Argentine gaucho poem *Martín Fierro*, several gangster movies, and, surprisingly, Joyce's *Ulysses*, which he sees as "an autonomous world of corroborations, of omens, of monuments" (79). It follows then that the effectiveness of the technique that he favors is not restricted to the adventure novel, since it is central also to one of the pillars of the modernist revolution. This supports indirectly Borges' rejection of the psychological novel as outmoded, and also of "natural" causality, which results from uncontrollable and infinite operations and is typical of the "psychological simulation" (ibid.) in which traditional novels are engaged. For the novel the only honest path, he concludes, is "magic causality."[3]

In the preface to his friend and collaborator Adolfo Bioy Casares'[4] novel *La invención de Morel* (1940), Borges expresses some of the preceding ideas more clearly. In this text he outlines a theory of fiction capable of refuting the importance of the psychological or realistic novel—as he had already attempted to do in "Narrative Art and Magic"—and of replacing it, as the best possible form of narrative, with the adventure story. This genre, by refraining from attempts to imitate reality, avoids the pitfalls of the typical psychological novel, which "tends to be amorphous. The Russians and their disciples have bored us," he goes on to say, "with demonstrations that nothing is impossible: people who commit suicide out of happiness, murderers who kill out of kindness, people who love each other so much that they part from each other forever, informants out of fervor and humility. . . . That total freedom ends up being the same as total disorder."[5]

Borges objects also to the psychological novel's pretension of being "realistic": "it prefers that we forget that it is by nature a verbal artifice [Borges' third collection of stories, later printed together with the second one, *Ficciones*, was titled *Artificios*[6]], and makes of every vain precision (or of every languid vagueness) a new touch of verisimilitude" (12). The focus of the essay previously discussed was the rejection of the causality depicted by the realistic novel in favor of a magical type of connection between reality and the unknown. *Morel's Invention*'s preface proceeds in a straightforward rather than a roundabout fashion to praise the adventure novel, without, however, linking it to magic or, by extension, to the fantastic.

The adventure novel is better equipped than any other form of fiction to demonstrate the artificiality which is intrinsic to fiction. Because it does not attempt a transcription of reality but is itself an artificial object that excludes all unnecessary elements, the adventure novel must, in order to avoid being repetitious (as happens in *The Golden Ass*, *Sinbad's Travels*, and *Don Quixote*), develop an extremely rigorous plot. With the evolution of literature, those plots have become increasingly sophisticated, so that, although Stevenson is a more lucid, passionate, and varied writer than Chesterton, the latter's plots are better, as are also Kafka's compared to De Quincey's (13). Contrary to what most people think, contemporary literature has produced better plots—i.e., more "artificial," and more "magic" too—than the literature of previous centuries. While claiming to be free from "the superstition of modernity" (ibid.) that believes that anything produced today is intrinsically better than that which was produced yesterday, Borges ends the essay by stating that in his opinion no other epoch can boast novels with such admirable plots as James' *The Turn of the Screw*, Kafka's *Der Prozess*, Julian Green's *Le voyageur sur la terre*, and the novel by Bioy Casares that he is introducing.

Before we return to this last statement, mention should be made of an unpublished lecture of 1949, in which Borges takes a look at the techniques (*procedimientos*) of fantastic literature.[7] These he reduces to four: the text within the text, contamination of reality by the dream, travel in time, and the double. A close look at the four texts which, in his preface to *Morel's Invention*, Borges claims exemplify the best possible plots that modern literature can produce, shows that techniques of the fantastic as he defines them are not present in all of them. *Le voyageur sur la terre* illustrates the last three devices mentioned by Borges; but only by stretching to the utmost the implications of the second one can it encompass *The Trial* as well as *Morel's Invention*; and "the text within the text" applies to *The Turn of the Screw* only in the strictly technical sense that the governess' memoir is presented as a text antedating the one into which it is introduced. Bioy Casares' novel could be construed to illustrate the *mise en abîme* or Chinese boxes technique ("the text within the text") in a purely metaphorical way: its protagonist inserts himself into the text—Morel's invention—which he is at the same time "reading," or, more accurately, seeing and listening to, since it is a movie.

If we look at these four narratives in relation to the characteristics of the fantastic as defined by Todorov, it turns out that only *The Turn of the Screw* features the hesitation regarding the reality of the supernatural which he defines as basic to the genre. It remains, nevertheless, a psychological novel, since regardless of whether the events narrated by the protagonist are accepted as having taken place or not, the emphasis of the narrative is on their effect on the mind of the governess. In *Le voyageur sur la terre*, an elusive and lyrical modernist novella which does employ most of the techniques that Borges cites as characteristic of fantastic literature, the reader realizes very soon—thus precluding Todorov's hesitation—that the strange events that besiege the protagonist are not to be taken literally, but as the representation of a higher order of perception that he has come in contact with. In *The Trial* everything is portrayed realistically, so that the contradictory, strange, and in the final account impossible quality of those events makes us look for explanations of them not in some conflicting reality within the text, but outside the text, in its author's purpose for writing it. There turn out to be many possible allegorical interpretations, since no single explanation of K's trial seems sufficient to fix the meaning of the novel. (Consequently, *The Trial* exemplifies the model for allegory praised by Borges in two essays of *Other Inquisitions*.)[8] In *Morel's Invention*, finally, the author provides, two-thirds of the way into the narrative, a supposedly scientific explanation of the mysterious, incomprehensible presence of the guests on the deserted island. That explanation brings the novel fully into the realm of science fiction.

One must conclude then that the only characteristic uniting for Borges these four favorite novels of his—a classically fantastic novella, an allegorical novel, a lyrical story of time travel, and a science fiction novel—is their having good—i.e., original—plots, a condition that Borges links to the adventure story while claiming at the same time that it is typical of all modern literature. Only by assuming that fantastic narratives are comprised within the adventure mode—an assumption contradicted by *The Turn of the Screw*, the only fantastic novel of the four cited by Borges—could we extend to them the principles described by Borges in those two essays.

Borges' inclusion of *Morel's Invention* in this list has the effect of presenting the three European texts as heralding Bioy Casares', which has, due to its being closer to the adventure tale, an even more original plot than the others. It should be stressed that none of these works rejects psychological characterization or ignores realistic description, although Borges' critique of the traditional novel in this same preface would lead us to believe that must be a condition for the excellence of the adventure novel. And as far as exemplifying a causality based on the "magic," arbitrary attraction or sympathy between nature's objects, only *Le voyageur* suggests such a connection. (*The Trial*'s plot follows a seemingly realistic causality, one, however, whose governing force cannot be identified.)

Are Borges' *ficciones* (a term coined by him that we are justified in extending to all the stories included in the books that followed the one bearing that title) adventure tales, fantastic stories, or perhaps allegories? It should be kept in mind in this respect that the type of allegory defended by Borges (see n. 29) is not the basically static one typical of medieval literature, but a more flexible, and in his view also more effective kind, capable of eliciting the type of multiple readings that Kafka's novels call for. Because they are meaning-suspended, those novels resist the sort of well-rounded definitions into which, notwithstanding their unquestionable richness and complexity, we are able to translate the meaning and intention of *The Divine Comedy* or *Piers Plowman*.

In the preface to *The Garden of Forking Paths*, Borges says, apologetically, that " 'The Babylon Lottery' is not completely innocent of symbolism" (*Ficciones* 11). And the story's readers will agree that the lottery that governs Borges' Babylon stands unmistakably for chance, while Babylon symbolizes the world, which, as everyone knows, is run by hazard. Chance seems also to characterize another representation of the world in the same collection, "The Library of Babel," whose opening line reads: "The universe (which others call the Library)" (85). The world, meaning the aggregate of human lives, is seen in these stories, respectively, as a vast game which through a series of steps has changed its rules to reproduce the disorder and unpredictability of nature, and as a library whose librarian-inhabitants search vainly for a meaning or an order that they believe must exist, in order to justify the creation of their world-library. That meaning, however, cannot ever be found in the infinite (because it is "periodic," as our planet would appear to be to those who cross it in the same direction more than once) library.

These stories are allegorical not in the narrow sense by which Beatrice, for example, translates only into faith, but in more complex and thought-provoking, and less easily defined ways. Borges' are, in other words, modern allegories. Yet they are basically straightforward ones—while at the same time intellectually rich—and as such, drastically different from Kafka's. This is, in turn, a consequence of their lack of novelistic substance. Borges' approach to fiction is based on avoiding psychological characterization (we saw how he criticized the novel for relying too much on this) and realistic detail, both of which make Kafka's obviously allegorical narratives markedly novelistic, thus helping to defer their meaning. But Borges' stories also tend to avoid the action that in the adventure novel should suggest "magic's mysterious causality."

None of the other seventeen stories that make up the two parts of *Ficciones* can be called allegorical in the strict sense of the term. In the 1941 preface already quoted, Borges says that all but one of the stories in *The Garden of Forking Paths* (the title story, which is a "detective story") are fantastic, a claim which implicitly includes "The Library of Babel" and "The Babylon Lottery" (about the latter, as we saw, he adds that it is partially symbolic). In the preface to *Artificios* (1944), the second part of *Ficciones*, Borges states that the stories in this group do not differ from the ones in the preceding collection. The author's 1949 epilogue to *The Aleph* says that except for "Emma Zunz" and "Tale of the Warrior and the Captive," the texts in that book belong to the fantastic genre.

If we take a close look at these stories, it becomes apparent that very few of them can justifiably be called fantastic, whether according to Todorov's identification of the genre with the hesitation provoked in the reader by the account of supernatural events, or according to those broader characterizations of the genre, including the ones that antedate Todorov's, that focus on the mere implausibility of the events narrated, i.e., on their being "fantastic," not just in the sense that they fall outside the laws of nature. Apart from the two stories just mentioned, the *Ficciones* stories that can with any degree of rigor be called "fantastic" are: "Tlön, Uqbar, Orbis Tertius" (the planet invented by a society of scholars begins to physically intrude in the real world); "Pierre Menard, Author of *Don Quixote*" (Menard is able to reproduce, word by word, some chapters of *Don Quixote* through an act of will); "The Circular Ruins" (the protagonist gives life to a man he has first dreamed, and discovers later that he too is someone else's dream); "Funes, the Memorious" (Funes is gifted—

or damned—with the capacity to remember, forever and in all its details, everything that he witnesses or reads); "The Secret Miracle" (the protagonist is granted by God a year to conclude, in his mind, the play he was writing at the time he was condemned to death; that year takes place in the second that elapses between the time when the firing squad fires at him and when the bullets reach him). And also, perhaps, "The Approach to Al-Mu'tasim" (this story pretends to be a review of a novel about a man's search for and eventual meeting with God). A total of five or six stories out of seventeen. The rest of them can be called "fantastic" only if we extend the meaning of the word all the way in the direction of its etymological identification with the imagination. But doing so can only succeed in depriving the concept of the fantastic of any usefulness as a critical tool for studying Borges' fiction.

Of *The Aleph*'s seventeen stories, Borges, as we just saw, identifies as "fantastic" fifteen of them. Taking as our principle for categorizing them the broader and more traditional view of the fantastic as simply the literary representation of the supernatural or the impossible, it becomes evident that only four of *The Aleph*'s stories really fit into the fantastic. These are: "The God's Script" (a magician is able to decipher his god's writing as inscribed in one of his creatures, a tiger); "The Immortal" (a man becomes immortal after drinking from a certain river, and then loses his immortality, many centuries later, by again drinking from the river); "The Other Death" (a man is granted by God the opportunity to re-enact the moment of his death through the modification of the recollection of it by all of its witnesses); "The Zahir" (the image of an apparently ordinary but in reality magic coin progressively takes over the whole thinking process of the protagonist-narrator); and the title story (named for an image of the universe, including the totality of its components perceived at once diachronically and synchronically, which is located—a tiny circle of light—in the staircase of a Buenos Aires cellar).

Writing about "Pierre Menard" in the prologue to the first part of *Ficciones*, Borges says that what is unreal in this story is the destiny that its protagonist chooses for himself. As students of contemporary literature know well, this story has become, since it was discussed first by the influential French writer Maurice Blanchot, and later by the critic Gérard Genette,[9] who interpreted it as a metaphor for the role of memory in relation to writing, a darling of post-structuralist criticism, and, for many a critic, Borges' archetypal text—which it may very well be, inasmuch as "Pierre Menard" argues for the impossibility of original creation. By proving that he can recreate a text not particularly dear to him, and one which, furthermore, he has partially forgotten, just by applying himself to the task with absolute thoroughness, Menard would like to demonstrate that literature is but a fabric of texts (or just words, as with the books that make up the library of Babel) belonging to all instead of to individual authors. (It should be noted, however, that the story's emphasis on the word-by-word likeness of Menard's *Quixote* to Cervantes'—it took him many years and thousands of drafts to write two chapters and part of another one—acts in fact against the concept, central to the post-modern attack on logocentrism, of writing as an interweaving of differences.)[10]

"Tlön, Uqbar, Orbis Tertius," which follows "Pierre Menard" in the chronology of Borges' writings,[11] ends with the account of how what was originally an ultra-sophisticated game for a few initiates—consisting in the elaboration in writing of a fictitious planet (Tlön), where philosophical idealism prevailed to the extent that it had actually affected reality—seems to have turned into an evil project aimed at dazzling the human mind (as has been done already by dialectical materialism, antisemitism, nazism). The result is that the history, philosophy and languages of that "Third World" (the "Orbis Tertius" of the story's title) whose first manifestation was the country of Uqbar, are rapidly replacing those of the real world. Thus, literature and the writer as the products of an individual vocation, which is how the Western mind has traditionally defined them, will become, due to the takeover of the world by the invented planet, a "vanishing peculiarity."[12] This is illustrated by the story-essay's author's description of how he persists, oblivious to the *Orbis Tertius* invasion, in revising, exclusively for his own pleasure (he does not plan to have it published), "a tentative translation in the style of Quevedo ... of Browne's *Urn Burial*" (*Ficciones* 34; my translation).

Menard's "experiment" aims at proving that "to think, to analyze, to invent ... are not extraordinary acts, but intelligence's normal breathing. To glorify the occasional fulfilling of that function, to treasure old and alien thoughts, to remember with incredulous awe what the *doctor universalis* thought is to confess our laziness or our stupidity. All men should be capable of thinking all the ideas, and I understand that it will be so in the future" (56). (This is exactly the future depicted in the story "Utopia of a Tired Man," from Borges' last collection.) That erasure of the individual writer corresponds rather exactly to what is practiced in Tlön, where "the idea of a unique subject" prevails, books are usually unsigned, the concept of plagiarism does not exist, it has been established that all texts are the work of a single author who is anonymous and exists outside time, and finally criticism invents authors and attributes to them very different works in order to determine the psychology of that "interesting *homme de lettres*" (27). Menard's writing of *Don Quixote* suggests to the narrator of "Pierre Menard" that we should engage in a similar game: "the technique of the deliberate anachronism and the erroneous attributions" enriches the "elementary art of reading" and "fills with adventure the dullest books by allowing us, for instance, to attribute to Céline or to Joyce the *Imitation of Christ*" (57).

It is obvious that "Tlön" includes a restatement of Menard's ideas regarding the abolition of individual authorship in the preceding description of the planet's "literary habits." The narrator's final comments on how he is facing the destruction of his entire world point, however, to something much more specific and historically determined: "Tlön" is a pessimistic reflection on the rise of nazism and its initial victories in the war that had begun in 1939.[13] Those concluding remarks by the narrator express the futility of the intellect in trying to counteract forces such as fascism (and also marxism) intent on destroying traditional values. Yet there is a powerful echo in them of Menard's convictions regarding the irrelevance of individual authorship (the narrator of "Tlön" is working on a translation into a style no longer practiced of a work that noone reads anymore), and, more to the point with respect to the historical grounding of the story in a chaotic present, of "Pierre Menard"'s pessimistic dismissal of the possibility of reaching others with our "message": only the friend of Menard's who writes the review article on him that we read has realized that Menard was not merely copying *Don Quixote*; and the narrator of "Tlön" is never going to have his translation published. While being undoubtedly poorer in philosophical implications regarding the art of writing than "Pierre Menard," "Tlön" is more effective as a short story from a traditional point of view, since it includes a good deal of action and even some characterization. It also falls much more comfortably within the fantastic genre due to its actual description of supernatural events and objects, namely the intrusion into the narrator's own environment of objects coming from Tlön: a compass that points south, a die-sized cone weighing hundreds of pounds.

In the preface to *The Garden of Forking Paths* Borges says of "The Circular Ruins" that in it "everything is unreal." And indeed it is, but not in the same sense in which a tale about supernatural events is "unreal." The story is another philosophical reflection on the same idea posited by "Pierre Menard": original creation is illusory, as Menard's act of will proves. In "Ruins," the magician's belief that his intellectual concentration has succeeded in creating a living being from nothingness is destroyed when he realizes that, since the fire that will not burn his "son" does not touch him either, he too is unreal, the creation of someone else's mind—obviously that of the story's author, Borges. "Ruins" is a metaphor of artistic creation, above and beyond its advancing of the notion that originality is not attainable.

"Funes, the Memorious" is described by Borges in the preface to *Artificios* as "an extended metaphor for insomnia." Funes has difficulty sleeping, and his infinite memory (the supernatural element in the story), described by him as "a garbage dump" (123), resembles the meaningless yet precise images that fill the mind during sleepless nights or when we are half asleep. For him who cannot sleep ("to withdraw—*distraerse*—from the world" [126] is how Borges defines sleep in the story), but who instead ceaselessly remembers every detail of the world around him, and the memory of those memories as well as of his readings, projects, and dreams, thinking becomes impossible, since thinking—and its corollary, creation—demand (and this is the story's point) that we "forget differences" and develop our capacity for "generalizing and for abstraction" (ibid.). Funes' infinite memory, first equated with insomnia, seems to prevent him not only from reaching "general, platonic ideas" (125), but also from thinking at all. This, in turn, might be attributed to the protagonist's humble origin (he is the son of a washerwoman) and lack of formal education, which make it impossible for him to take advantage—assuming that this would have been possible—of his magic gift. Funes sees only details; all he can do, besides devising some crazy systems for giving names to numbers and for classifying all his memories, is to review those same details. Menard, on the other hand, had first, in order to appropriate Cervantes' *Quixote*, to forget it.[14]

"The Secret Miracle" too introduces the supernatural into the realm of reality, in this case through the conversion by God of a second into a year. This event is described, however, without underlining its impossibility, and contrary to what was done in "Tlön," which employed the device of bringing into the everyday world the fictitious planet's objects. The supernatural takes place in "The Secret Miracle" without being witnessed by anyone besides the protagonist and recipient of the miracle, and exclusively within his mind. This suggests that we read the story not as the fantastic narrative that to a certain extent it is, but as yet another reflection on or metaphor for writing. The writer condemned to die by the Nazis (another manifestation of those same evil powers that threaten traditional values through Tlön's invasion of our planet) is given a chance to complete the play he was working on at the time of his arrest. This he does solely for his own satisfaction, since this drama through which he had hoped to redeem himself from a "vague literary career" (160) will never be known to the outside world and will remain in fact unwritten: it exists only in the protagonist's memory as the mentally spoken words of a drama in verse. The formal perfection of it ("Hladík disposed of no other way of recording but his own memory; learning each new hexameter had luckily imposed on him a rigor not suspected by those who introduce and then forget whole paragraphs which are vague and superfluous" [166]) tends to confirm the Platonic claim that memory, and by extension the pursuit of knowledge, were forever undermined by the invention of writing.[15] But in fact it suggests an alternative to the dichotomy between the traditionally favored oral sign and the written one, since the play is completed by *inscribing* the sign on its author's memory instead of on paper. Like the translation of Browne's *Urn Burial* that the narrator of "Tlön" is doing, his back turned to the foreign planet's intrusion into his world, and like Menard's *Quixote* too, Hladík's drama, *The Enemies*, will remain unknown, confirming once again the ultimate futility of intellectual enterprises—as does also "The Circular Ruins" by showing that the magician's laborious creation is but a dream dreamt by a dream.

"The Immortal" resembles "The Secret Miracle" in that it does not include a single witness (an essential element of the fantastic for Todorov) of the supernatural other than the immortal himself. And indeed, the account of his own life by Joseph Cartaphilus that makes up most of the story's text could be entirely false—as the "1950 Postscriptum" to the story by the outside narrator who introduced the protagonist's manuscript tells us one critic claims it is, thus pointing to the way the narrative appropriates, without acknowledging their origin, fragments by other writers.

The purpose of the story becomes clear in its last paragraph: "The Immortal" is designed to show how, as our end approaches, all that is left is not images or memories, but words, "displaced and mutilated words, words by others" (*El aleph* 26). Thus Cartaphilus does not have to be physically immortal in order to achieve immortality. (Conversely, Menard had remarked that his project was not difficult in itself, only that one would need to be immortal to achieve it [51].) By appropriating, whether deliberately or unconsciously, the words, and through them also the memories of a chain of writers that extends from Homer to Bernard Shaw, the protagonist has become immortal. And he has also restated Menard's conclusion that the written text (but perhaps not the one that remains entirely in the writer's mind, like Hladík's) belongs to anyone capable of re-enunciating it.

"The Aleph" is clearly about literary creation rather than about the existence of a magic window-compendium of the universe in a Buenos Aires basement. At the end of the story its narrator, Borges, our only witness to the aleph, asks himself whether the aleph he saw, which has now been erased by the demolition of the building where it stood, was the real one or just another in a long series of false alephs (which he proceeds to enumerate according to the scholarly sources that describe them). And finally he wonders whether perhaps he did see the *real* aleph when he saw everything in the universe, and has now forgotten it, in the same way that he is already confusing, and will ultimately lose with the passage of time, the memory of the face of Beatriz (a woman whom he loved and in whose house the aleph was located).

These comments result in undermining to a considerable extent the story's fantastic effect. They also help to reveal what it is really about. Like "The Circular Ruins," "The Aleph" is an image of literary creation. The impossibility that through a tiny sphere one could see the whole universe moving through time (as in a movie, and more specifically in those newsreels of the forties called "The March of Time") suggests that only literature can provide such a window into the universe, since only literature possesses the capacity to evoke all the richness and variety of the world. This is demonstrated by the effectiveness with which the narrator describes what he saw in the aleph: "I saw the teeming sea; I saw daybreak and nightfall; I saw the multitudes of America; I saw a silvery cobweb in the center of a black pyramid; I saw a splintered labyrinth (it was London); I saw, close up, unending eyes watching themselves in me as in a mirror; I saw all the mirrors on earth and none of them reflected me . . ." (*Aleph and Other Stories* 27).

Thus an aleph (the first letter of the sacred alphabet, the pure divinity) would be not only unnecessary but actually a hindrance to the imaginative powers of a writer, since it would tie him to what is reflected in that mirror—to the realistic description abhorred by Borges—instead of fostering the use of his imagination to evoke, as it is his task to do, the universe. "The Aleph" expresses rather coherently the art called for by Borges' poetics, which can be characterized as an art of allusion.[16] At the same time, it is a vehicle for satirizing the opposite technique, description, the one that the silly Carlos Argentino Daneri, Beatriz' cousin and lover (as the narrator finds out thanks to the aleph), and the tenant of the house where the aleph is located, employs in attempting to "sing" in a poem the whole earth just as he sees it day after day through his private window. As in so many Borges stories, this too includes a pessimistic comment on the fate of "good literature": while the narrator's poems do not receive a single vote in the competition for the National Literary Award, Carlos Argentino's work wins the second prize.

"The Zahir" seems a more traditional type of fantastic story. The supernatural coin that absorbs, by entirely occupying it, the mind of the narrator-protagonist (Borges, as in "The Aleph") reveals its obsession-producing nature slowly. The existence of objects endowed with the power to produce an obsession capable of entirely absorbing a man's mind is confirmed by a learned monograph on "the superstition of the Zahir," and immediately following this, by the protagonist's discovery that there are other people in Buenos Aires afflicted by his illness. Imagining then the terrible fate that awaits him when he becomes totally possessed by the image of the coin, the narrator reflects: "When everyone on earth thinks day and night of the zahir, which one will be the dream and which one the reality, the earth or the zahir?" And later on: "Perhaps I will end up spending it [the coin] entirely through thinking and rethinking it constantly; perhaps God is behind the coin" (*El aleph* 113-14).

By assuming that at some time everybody on earth may suffer from his obsession, something which, in turn, may have been divinely ordained as a way for men "to get lost" in God, the narrator is foreseeing a world very much like the one projected in "Tlön" once everything in the universe is under the control of the invented planet. In that new world, as we saw, there would be no place left for the intellectual as we traditionally conceive of him. In "The Zahir" that same intellectual has not given up hope entirely regarding the meaningfulness of his labors, but he is already incapacitated for work because of the absorption of his mind by a vulgar object. The obsession produced by the zahir resembles Funes' equally obsessive memory, which, like the zahir, precludes rest and forgetfulness and, consequently, creativity and the fruitful development of the imagination as well. ("The Aleph" 's protagonist, on the other hand, after fearing that once he saw the aleph everything in the universe would look familiar to him—this would be equivalent to not being able to forget anything—begins to forget what he saw.)

Although much lighter in tone and intellectual content than the other meta-literary stories discussed above, "The Zahir" points also to the bleak future that awaits intellectuals in the modern world as pictured in "Tlön." In other words, we remain in this story—the presence of the supernatural in it notwithstanding—firmly within the arena of commentary on artistic, and more specifically, literary creativity.

"The Other Death" also seems at first to be a traditional fantastic story. Pedro Damián, who had behaved cowardly in a battle that took place during the civil wars in Uruguay at the beginning of the century, revives at the moment of his death in the same battle, and dies in it again, but now as the most courageous of soldiers ("as any man would like to die" [747]). God, rewarding Damián for his dedication to erasing the bad memory of his cowardice ("he never lifted a hand against another man, he never cut anyone up, he never sought fame as a man of courage. Instead, living out there in the hill country of Ñancay and struggling with the backwoods and with wild cattle, he made himself tough, hard" [*The Aleph* 109]), modifies the image of him in the memories of those survivors of the battle who formerly remembered him as a coward, so they now think that he died a hero. And God also erases the memory of Damián in those who knew him after he settled in Entre Ríos, where the narrator, who is ostensibly Borges, met him; he already has great difficulty remembering him.

If the story had concluded with the "explanation" of the miracle performed by God in relation to Damián's death, it would fall rather neatly within Todorov's category of the supernatural accepted. After presenting the mystery and exploring various possible explanations of it, some of which are rational (there are two Damiáns, the one who died in the battle and the one who died in his bed; the narrator dreamed the first one), and pointing to what makes these unsatisfactory, two supernatural explanations are introduced in order of increasing complexity, the second eventually being accepted by the narrator as the true one. The conclusion is that the laws of nature were suspended for a while.

But this kind of fantastic ending does not satisfy Borges. The narrator had begun to make inquiries regarding Damián because the news of his death, which supposedly took place as he was mentally reliving the famous battle of Masoller, has suggested to him writing a fantastic story about that battle (notice, by the way, the contradiction involved—no doubt deliberately—in twice interviewing veterans of the battle of Masoller in order to ask for data on it with the purpose of writing a fantastic story about that battle). The narrator reflects at the end that his discovery of the miracle is not as extraordinary (and thus not as fearful: the shopkeeper who knew the "real" Damián has died "because he had too many memories" [78] of him) as it seemed at first. It is, after all, made of false memories. In the first place, Pedro Damián "(if indeed he lived)" (79) must have been called something else, the name "Pedro Damián" being the narrator's unconscious way of making himself believe that the story he just told us was suggested to him by the arguments of Pier Damiani (to which he was led, in turn, by two verses on a problem of identity in the *Divine Comedy*) sustaining that God can cause to be that which never was. The poem mentioned at the very beginning of the story (Emerson's "The Past"), in connection with but apparently unrelated to Damián's death, is not a casual choice either, since it deals with the irreversibility of the past.

The lines that follow in the text affirm the reality of the miracle: "By 1951 I shall think that I composed a fantastic story, but I will have recorded a historical event; just as some two thousand years ago Virgil, in all innocence, thought that he was announcing the birth of a man and not foretelling that of God" (79). But what precedes this sentence, the turning inside out of the supernatural, has already succeeded in dismantling the fantastic effect by exposing the artistic process by which the author arrived at the final product.[17]

"The Other Death" recalls those stories such as Nerval's *Aurélia* and James' *The Turn of the Screw* which for Todorov exemplify the best of the fantastic in that they are able to sustain for the longest possible period of time the uncertainty paradigmatic of the genre. But that resemblance to the genre's classics is only apparent. What Borges wishes to accomplish by discussing the various possibilities related to Pedro Damián's death and the way that others remember it is not simply to envelop in ambiguity both the rational and the supernatural explanations of his death. The story does achieve this, but only laterally and as a critical afterthought; the author is more interested in playing at revealing his literary devices. This seems a natural consequence of a writer's technique having achieved its full maturity, as was the case with Borges' by the time of *The Aleph*'s publication. Furthermore, Borges was by then about to stop writing stories (let us now call them "fantastic" for the sake of expediency) of the sort to which "The Other Death" belongs.[18] Thus he decided to reveal, for his own amusement, the elements with which he had worked, and which made it possible for him to write this text. These prove to be not the barbarous battle of Masoller, regardless of the attraction that primitive courage held for Borges, but the *Divine Comedy*, some theological arguments, a poem by Emerson—some of the elements, in other words, that make up his literary and philosophical culture. The fantastic quality of the story is thus effectively weakened and even effaced for the sake of exposing the intellectual framework of the tale.

"The God's Script" is very similar thematically to "The Secret Miracle": an imprisoned Aztec priest tries to discover the magic words which, uttered by his god, would put an immediate end to his imprisonment.[19] (Hladík, also a political prisoner, is addressed by God in a dream in response to his plea to extend his life.) In "The God's Script," before the sacred sentence is revealed to the supplicant at the end of a dream that becomes a mystic experience, he is united with his god, a just reward for his devotion and long sufferings (the protagonist of "The Secret Miracle" is an agnostic). As a consequence, the priest gives up his project of freeing himself and restoring the Aztec Empire—although he now has the means to do so—as too banal an enterprise in view of his new spiritual state. This decision is philosophically similar to Hladík's conviction that completing his play is important only for himself.

As in "The Secret Miracle," there are no witnesses to this miracle other than its recipient, thus helping to eliminate any kind of hesitation regarding the appearance of the supernatural and calling instead for its acceptance without question. On the other hand, in "The God's Script," as in the *Ficciones* story, we could easily dismiss the magician's revelation, of which he is the sole witness and teller, as an hallucination or a dream. The fact that "The Secret Miracle" 's protagonist is an intellectual, the psychological complexity of the play he composes, and the tension that its composition creates between speech and writing all give that story a depth that "The God's Script" lacks. Although this story too has at its center a piece of writing, writing in it is only an element of a beautifully described, but on the whole not very original, mystical experience. It should also be noted that the priest's renunciation, after experiencing God, of his desire to avenge himself and his people on the Spanish conquerors may be read as suggesting that any criticism of the Conquest is not worth the trouble. This is particularly disturbing considering that the man to whom the priest refers is Alvarado, who carried out the cruel and unprovoked massacre of the *Templo Mayor*.

The Borges stories that I have discussed so far in relation to the fantastic are those in which something supernatural occurs, those in which an event that defies natural laws takes place within a world that otherwise reproduces, albeit in the sparing way characteristic of Borges' technique, the real world. As we have seen, a close and objective reading of those stories shows that in all of them the supernatural element—Menard's success in rewriting, word for word, some chapters of *Don Quixote*; Funes' total memory; Tlön's mysterious objects; the zahir; the aleph; the dreamed men of "The Circular Ruins"; God's writing; the miracle granted to the writer Hladík; or the shifting recollections of Pedro Damián by those who knew him—is not the actual subject of the story, but merely a device used to develop the real subject. The real subjects of these stories are, of course, artistic creation and intellectual pursuits, and, ultimately, the future of such pursuits in relation to what Borges perceives as the decline of Western civilization.

In these stories the supernatural element is not intended to produce the effect that it is designed to achieve in the fantastic. The supernatural in them does not frighten or even surprise us much, in part because in most cases it does not take place suddenly, but rather is simply introduced as a given fact. And, more importantly, the supernatural occurrence does not, as a rule, provoke any hesitation as to whether or not it could have actually taken place. This is so because the contrast between the impossible element and normal reality is not emphasized after the initial presentation but is rather de-emphasized through the development of its value as a literary device and (in one case) the discussion of its provenance. Borges' "fantastic" stories (those that include a supernatural event) belong most comfortably within Todorov's category of the "marvelous accepted," as do Kafka's narratives.

Only in "Tlön" does the appearance of the supernatural have a decidedly haunting effect, though this is not insisted upon. The compass, and even more so the impossibly heavy cone found in a Brazilian jungle, possess the concreteness typical of the objects of the fantastic, thus bringing this story—in many ways Borges' most intellectual *ficción*, due to its reliance on philosophical arguments—closest to the fantastic genre at a certain, crucial level. The forever unexplained nature of those objects, recalled again by the narrator toward the end of his account,[20] fascinates us and actually stirs in our minds the "fantastic doubt": could Tlön, after all, be real?

Because it is so paradigmatic of Borges' overall production, I have left until the end discussing "The Approach to Al-Mu'tasim," one of his earliest short stories, and the first in the style that would make him famous.[21] "Al-Mu'tasim" is not really a fantastic story, but it is close enough to the genre to permit us to read it as part of the fantastic by forgetting momentarily the distinction between the story that is told and the frame that encloses it. The story concerns a student's search for God, whose reflection he detects (like the intervention of "a more complex interlocutor" in a dialogue [*Ficciones* 39]) in one of the many despicable men that he meets in the course of his travels through India. His search leads him to Al-Mu'tasim, at the luminous threshold of whose room the narrative ends.

If the description of the protagonist's journey constituted the whole text, the short story would fall neatly within the fantastic, since it introduces the existence of the supernatural. The pilgrimage, however, is not the subject of the story proper, but of a fictitious—and apparently fantastic—novel, *The Approach to Al-Mu'tasim*, the subject in turn of "The Approach to Al-Mu'tasim,'' a short story that adopts the form of a book review of that novel. And the review, after telling the plot of the invented novel, criticizes it thoroughly, especially in its second version, called *A Game of Shifting Mirrors*. The reviewer behind whom Borges hides accuses his subject of overdoing the expected allegorical meaning of such a story (man's search for God takes place within himself) and then looks for the novel's sources and lesser known antecedents. In other words, "The Approach to Al-Mu'tasim" tells a fantastic story and then destroys the fantastic effect provoked by it. The same happens, in less direct ways, in others of Borges' *ficciones* which play with the fantastic for a while and then go on to suggest an allegorical reading of themselves ("Tlön"), or to develop the intellectual implications of the supernatural element ("Pierre Menard," "Funes," "The Zahir"), sometimes extending in the direction of a commentary on the writing of fiction ("The Circular Ruins," "The Immortal," "The Aleph"). "The Other Death," finally, is basically about the writing of a fantastic story, as is also Borges' earliest work in the genre, "The Approach to Al-Mu'tasim," a story about a seemingly fantastic novel which turns out to be as allegorical (although in a cruder, more obvious way) as two of his later stories, "The Babylon Lottery" and "The Library of Babel."

As I have suggested, the critique which in "Al-Mu'tasim" appears aimed at the allegorical intention of the invented novel, and which in the process of making fun of it destroys the fantastic effect created by the narrative (the description of the protagonist's hearing Al-Mu'tasim's voice and entering his room is quite powerful)[22] would, in his later work become the trademark of Borges' approach to the fantastic and to storytelling in general. This technique, often carried out in a sort of epilogue to the story, consists in describing the apparent subject of the narrative from the detached perspective of a critic who reviews erudite sources on it and/or comments on its philosophical implications. This is equivalent to dismantling the action of the story and destroying its drama, and with it, in those stories that deal with the supernatural, the hesitation characteristic of the fantastic. By proceeding in this manner Borges brings to the forefront, in case the reader has overlooked it, the intellectual substance of the story, which is, for him, its main reason for being. It is no wonder then that Pierre Menard, that Borgesian paradigm of the intellectual pursuit, should choose as the proof that he is capable of writing the *Quixote*, the ninth chapter of the first part, which introduces Cide Hamete Benengeli, the Arabic "author" of the story of don Quixote, through whom Cervantes expresses his own detachment from his creation.

Although it has been said many times, it bears repeating in the context of this analysis, that the stories by Borges that we have been discussing are *metafictions*. In them the *story* is, more pointedly than in other fiction (except, of course, in allegories), a vehicle for the *récit* to transcend and transform in order to deal as quickly as possible (without stopping to develop characterization, human relations, setting) with the preoccupations, mostly philosophical in nature, that are the origin of the story.

Curiously enough, it is in the stories that include a fantastic element that we most often encounter such reflection on literature, although this does occur in quite a few of Borges' stories that do not include the supernatural but are clearly *metafictions* too. Some of the stories studied in the preceding pages ("The Circular Ruins," "Pierre Menard," "Tlön") are of an even more sparse, linear nature than is usual in Borges; but even in those texts in which realistic detail and characterization play some role ("Funes," and especially "The Aleph"), they are not in fact of much concern to the writer, who remains in both types of stories basically unencumbered by reality and thus free to develop fully the super-text that is his real concern from the very beginning. The supernatural elements in the stories just discussed serve as a mediator that turns the narrative away from dealing with reality, in the direction of a meditation on literature. In the case of "The Aleph," the fantastic element becomes by its very nature an ideal vehicle to develop such a meditation.

It is important to note how superbly "readable" both Borges' fantastic and his non-fantastic stories are. Contrary to much postmodern fiction (of which Borges is supposed to be one of the founders), whose self-reflexivity, playfulness, and fondness for structural experimentation very often detract from the pleasure that reading it should afford, Borges' *ficciones* keep their readers' attention from beginning to end, even in subsequent readings. This seems to be a consequence of their having excellent plots—as Borges claimed *Morel's Invention*, and all modern fiction, did. A second look, however, reveals that Borges' *ficciones* actually feature potentially superb plots—superb often as plots for adventure-type stories, but just as often for psychological narratives—which are, however, not allowed to develop that potential lest this should interfere with the story's ability to express, as succinctly and quickly as possible, certain ideas. That this is the writer's principal goal does not diminish, however, the plot's hold on the readers' interest. This is so because its potential richness, although never expanded, is also never diminished by the pursuit of more or less philosophical reflections; it is actually enhanced by being kept undeveloped, and made even more suggestive. Borges' facility at inventing plots is such that in several of his stories he describes in a few sentences words of superb richness.[23] Because, as he said in the preface to *The Garden of Forking Paths*: "It is a tiresome and impoverishing madness to write long books, to elaborate in five hundred pages an idea whose perfect oral exposition takes a few minutes. A better procedure is to pretend that those books already exist and offer a synthesis of them, a comment" (*Ficciones* 11).

Borges is a born novelist who has systematically refused to write a novel. This follows directly from his attitude toward characterization, which in his view creates nothing but confusion while aiming at reproducing reality. Although it plays a minimum role in those four masterpieces mentioned by Borges at the end of his introduction to *Morel's Invention*, characterization is present in all of them, being an unavoidable element of any novel, a function of thematic complexity and mere length. Characterization, however, can be minimized and even ignored altogether in the short story, which is what happens in Borges' *ficciones*.

It is because of the importance that he gives to the adventure novel as ideally suited (because it does not pretend to mimic reality, but openly acknowledges its own "artificial" character) to develop absorbing plots, that Borges makes use so often of detective story-like structures for his short stories. But the truth is that texts like "The Garden of Forking Paths" or "Death and the Compass" can be called detective stories only in a very loose way. Although their apparent structure is that of a simple *cuento policial*, in fact they are not concerned with what interests traditional detective fiction, i.e., the solution of a crime. These stories are not *metaficciones* in the same sense that other "canonical" Borges stories are, but they too aim to go beyond their own plots in order to depict the strangeness of a chaotic world. They belong within what has been called "metaphysical detective fiction" (Holquist, "Whodunit").

In his next two books of stories, *Doctor Brodie's Report* and *The Book of Sand*, Borges deals with the supernatural in a manner different from that of what we may call his canonical texts. In the preface to *Doctor Brodie's Report*, Borges describes the stories included in that collection as "straightforward" (*directos*). They are not, however, "simple; there isn't anywhere on earth a single page or a single word that is, since each thing implies the universe, whose most obvious quality is complexity" (*El informe* 7). *Doctor Brodie*'s stories, "like those of the *Thousand and One Nights*, try to be entertaining or moving but not persuasive," and apart from the title story, they are all "realistic," i.e., they follow "the conventions of that genre. . . . They are rich in the required invention of circumstances" (9). Because he has given up writing "in a baroque style" to find, finally, his "own voice," these stories also avoid the surprises afforded by an unforeseen ending, preferring instead "to develop an expectation rather than to provide a startling shock" (10).

These remarks, which could be extended to the stories of the next collection, *The Book of Sand*, apply also to the fantastic stories contained in both books. These are not—as a consequence of their directness and, even more, of their striving above all to entertain—metaliterary, except in a rather derivative way ("The Book of Sand"). Nor is their reflexivity of a sort that could justify calling them philosophical, as is the case with some of the fantastic stories in *Ficciones* and *The Aleph*. The same can be said of the non-fantastic stories in Borges' last two books. In those that feature a speculative tone, the preoccupations stem, basically, with the exception of the title story in *Doctor Brodie*, from immediate concerns; the emphasis is on psychological description ("The Duel," "Guayaquil," "The Congress," "The Bribe"). Only one story, "The Gospel According to Mark," from *Doctor Brodie*, can be called metaliterary, and this in a very indirect way. [24]

The sole story of *Doctor Brodie* in which the supernatural plays a role is "The Meeting." The "meeting" of the title is that of two daggers that had belonged to two toughs of local Buenos Aires fame who hated each other. Placed by chance in the hands of two fashionable young men who have never before fought with knives (they are fighting ostensibly to settle an argument about gambling, but in reality because of an old grudge whose nature is never revealed), the daggers become, literally, alive: the hands of the two fighters shake as they grab them. Having begun to fight clumsily, the men find themselves very soon handling their daggers with masterful skill, and eventually, the weaker of the two men kills his opponent. The narrator, who had witnessed the event as a young boy in 1910 (Borges was then eleven years old), and explains around 1929[25] what really happened, concludes that what he watched "was the end of another story, an older story" (*El informe* 60), the one concerning the hatred between the two ruffians who never had the opportunity to meet each other in a fight.

As in many traditional fantastic stories, we have here a witness to the intrusion of the supernatural within the narrative. This is our narrator, someone very much like Borges himself: a member of the Buenos Aires upperclass born around the same time that he was, who has a cousin, as he did, called Lafinur (See "Autobiographical Essay," *The Aleph* 210), and is interested in turn-of-the century toughs of the Buenos Aires outskirts. Contrary to what normally happens in the fantastic, this witness does not see anything strange in the duel. The memory of it, however, often comes back to him. It is only after a former police officer to whom he tells the story reveals to him the daggers' pedigrees, that the narrator puts together the facts that explain as supernatural what took place: that is why "Uriarte's wrist shook, that is why Duncan's wrist shook. The two—[the daggers], not the men, their instruments—knew how to fight" (*El informe* 60).[26]

Of course, the reader may refuse to accept this interpretation, which might be why the English version of the story[27] stresses the possibility of a realistic instead of a magical explanation by saying: "I began to wonder whether it was Maneco Uriarte who killed Duncan or whether in some uncanny way it could have been the weapons, not the men, which fought" (*Doctor Brodie* 78), whereas the Spanish original translates literally as "Maneco Uriarte did not kill Duncan; the weapons, not the men, were the ones who fought. They had slept side by side in a cabinet until the hands woke them up" (*El informe* 60).

Much more so in the original than in its English version, "The Meeting" ends up in Todorov's category of the marvelous accepted, just like the "fantastic" stories previously discussed, except that "The Meeting" underlines, by discussing it, the occurrence of the supernatural. Once this is accepted, no matter how tentatively, the narrator moves out of it and concludes the story in the tone of meditative commentary that best characterizes Borges' fiction: "In their steel [the daggers'] slept and awaited [*acechaba*] human hatred. [This phrase is missing from the English translation.] Things last longer than people. Who knows if the story ends here, who knows if the daggers will not meet again" (61).

In the preface to *Doctor Brodie* Borges says that two of the stories in the collection "hold the same fantastic key" (10). (The original says, much less assertively, that they "allow for [*admiten*] the same fantastic key" [97].) The story with which "The Meeting" is paired, and which follows it in both the Spanish and English versions of *Doctor Brodie* (the stories in the English version do not follow exactly the order of the original) is "Juan Muraña." Although Borges says in the Afterword to *Doctor Brodie* that the "hidden link" between the two stories "is the fancy that a weapon, in time, may have a secret life of its own," that "a man, after death [could become] a thing . . . a knife fighter . . . his knife" (124), "Juan Muraña" does not include the supernatural at all. It is the story of a half-mad woman, the widow of a famous tough, Muraña,[28] who kills, using her late husband's knife, the landlord who is threatening to evict her, her sister, and her nephew,[29] believing all the time that it is Juan Muraña who saves them. There is no suggestion at all in the text that the woman's conviction is anything but a delusion fabricated by her madness; and in fact the narrator states in his conclusion that it was she who killed the landlord with "the dagger [that] was Muraña—it was the dead man she had gone on worshipping" (*Doctor Brodie* 86). One would have to move entirely outside of what the text of the story says, in the straightforward manner announced in the preface to the book, to be able to establish a link, supernaturally guided, between those three knives, as the Afterword suggests. The connection between the two stories, the "secret key" that opens up their meaning is, ultimately, not of a fantastic kind, but of the speculative, philosophical type that Borges favors. Its intention is to deindividualize people in favor of things: Juan Muraña "was a man who knew what all men come to know, a man who tasted death and was afterwards a knife, and is now the memory of a knife, and will tomorrow be oblivion—the oblivion that awaits us all" (ibid.).

Borges describes *The Book of Sand* (1975) in the "Note" to its English version in terms reminiscent of those that he used to talk about *Doctor Brodie's Report*. The new stories are but "variations on favorite themes"; they use "a plain and at times almost colloquial style" (*Book of Sand* 7). While introducing the previous collection of stories, Borges had singled out only two of them as being fantastic. Writing about *The Book of Sand*, he implies that all the stories in the new book belong (as he had said of the ones that made up *The Aleph*) to the fantastic genre: "I have tried to be faithful to the example of H. G. Wells in combining a plain and at times almost colloquial style with a fantastic plot" (7).

The Book of Sand includes Borges' first approximation to the horror tale, "There Are More Things" (in English in the original), dedicated, very appropriately, to a master of that genre, H. P. Lovecraft.[30] This is a sort of new version of the story "The House of Asterion," of *The Aleph*. The focus has switched from the Minotaur living in a labyrinth-like house[31] where he awaits the coming of the killer who will redeem him from his torment (as he also "frees" of all evils the men and women who are sacrificed to him), to the house itself. This is the monstrous, unimaginable mansion of a monster even more difficult to picture, with whose first steps—before he can be seen, and thus before anything supernatural has actually taken place—the story ends, provoking in the reader the expected goose flesh.

In *The Book of Sand* we find also Borges' first science fiction story. "Utopia of a Tired Man" belongs to the utopian branch of that genre. It gives us yet another version of our writer, this time as Eudoro Acevedo (the surname of Borges' mother), who was born in Buenos Aires two years before Borges actually was, and is, as Borges had been, a professor of English and American literature and a writer of fantastic ("imaginative" in the English version) tales. The story narrates Acevedo's visit in the *pampa* with a man from the future. To Acevedo's pessimistic description of our times as being filled with empty pursuits and dominated by the media, his host responds by telling him how much things have changed centuries later. There are no longer any cities, poverty as well as wealth has been eradicated, and since printing has been abolished, books are written by hand, and people, who speak Latin again, read very few of them. History, dates, facts, are not remembered; the people of the future are taught only to doubt "and the art of forgetting . . . what is personal and local" (91). And, as Borges had wished in the preface to *Doctor Brodie's Report*, there are no longer any governments ("I believe that some day we will deserve not to have governments" [10]).

This is a situation directly opposite that depicted in other futuristic texts, such as Eugene Zamiatin's *We*, Aldous Huxley's *Brave New World*, or George Orwell's *1984*, in which an overpowering universal government has crushed or is trying to crush all remaining traces of individual freedom. The conclusion of "Utopia," however, is as bleak as that reached in the novels just mentioned: Borges' men of the future, who are apparently immortal (the one the narrator meets is four hundred years old), father only one child, when they reach the century, and then, being ready to face their own selves and their "loneliness," devote themselves to "one of the arts or philosophy or mathematics or [play] a game of solitary chess" (94), until they decide to kill themselves. They do this by walking into a crematory's lethal chamber (it is not clear whether they do so carrying with them all their possessions—which are objects that they have made themselves, from kitchen utensils to paintings—or they give these away to friends), "said to have been invented by a philanthropist whose name, I think, was Adolf Hitler" (96). That suicide expresses their conviction that "there is no reason to carry on the human race," to the extent that many argue for "the advantages and disadvantages of gradual or simultaneous suicide" (93).

From its first lines, "Utopia" throws its readers into the realm of the supernatural without creating any hesitation as to its reality. This is so because the story employs the fantastic merely as a vehicle for conveying a pessimistic vision of human fate, which is but a darker manifestation of the ideology that informed "Tlön." It seems that even after governments and individual property have been eliminated, allowing each man to cultivate fully his intelligence, neither happiness nor (and this expresses even better Borges' view of the human race) communion between men is possible. Quite the contrary, isolation from each other appears to have been intensified.[32]

There are other stories in *The Book of Sand* that may be considered fantastic. "The Other," the first story in the collection, is described by Borges in the Afterword as dealing with "the old theme of the double" (123). He says that he tried to make sure that the two "speakers" in the story "were sufficiently different to be two persons, and alike enough to be one" (ibid.). "The Other" is an evocation of the writer's former self as a young man in Geneva (where he lived between 1914 and 1919), developed mainly with the purpose of contrasting the ideas of the young and the old Borges. This is accomplished by acquainting the former, sitting on a bench by the river Rhône in Geneva, with the ideas of the latter, who is sitting on that same bench, but facing the Charles River as it flows by the Harvard campus. The old Borges' characteristically reactionary views on history,[33] his elitism and militant individualism are rather thoroughly opposed to his former persona's convictions. The young Borges, we learn, loved Dostoevsky (whose approach to realism the mature author would mock in the preface to *Morel's Invention*), wanted to invent new metaphors, believed in "the brotherhood of man" (*Book of Sand* 14), and wanted to sing of this theme and of the oppressed.[34]

Since Borges would like to present this conversation with the person he used to be as a fantastic story, he makes the characters examine various ways of checking whether their meeting is taking place in reality or only in the mind of one of them—which is what the narrator eventually concludes. The discussion of the "reality" of the meeting only serves to undermine its fantastic character. Borges even introduces the notion of fear, so basic to the fantastic: "All this is a miracle, and the miraculous is terrifying" (18), says the young Borges. But since in fact there is nothing scary about the meeting, his future self explains that "the supernatural, if it occurs twice [the two dreams] ceases to be terrifying" (19). "The Other" is, notwithstanding Borges' effort to make it look like a traditional fantastic story, merely an excuse for an excursion into his own biography and ideological evolution.

"Ulrike" is a love story, whose unusualness within Borges' opus is noted in the Afterword: "The theme of love is quite common in my poems but not in my prose, which offers no other example than 'Ulrike' " (123). It also suggests the fantastic—which is why the Afterword notes a "formal affinity" between this story and "The Other" (124). "Ulrike" describes the meeting, in York, of a South American scholar and a Norwegian woman, their walk through the English woods once ruled by the Norwegians, and their lovemaking in "The Northern Inn" under the names of Sigurd and Brynhild. The action of the story is enveloped in a dreamlike atmosphere, but there is nothing supernatural in it; the dream is that of Borges the Anglophile admirer of Scandinavian sagas, as the last sentence of the text makes explicit: "In the darkness, centuries old, love flowed, and for the first and last time I possessed Ulrike's image" (25).

"The Disk" is related in the Afterword to the story "The Book of Sand": the two stories are about "two opposite and inconceivable concepts" (125). In "The Disk" the central concept is "the Euclidian circle, which has only one side" (ibid.). "The Disk" seems a rather straightforward fantastic story. The supernatural is introduced and accepted without question, in the form of the magic disk that the protagonist-narrator saw once and is still looking for many years after having killed its owner. The fact, however, that the story is told in the style of a legend, and that it takes place in a still Germanic England, with a woodcutter and a dethroned king as its characters, detracts from its fantastic effect and pushes the story instead into the realm of the mythical, the legendary, or simply the marvelous. Were it not for what the Afterword says about it, one would think that this was but the rewriting of an episode from an old chronicle or saga, as "The Sect of the Thirty," "The Mirror and the Mask," and "Undr," all in the same collection, pretend to be.

"The Book of Sand," finally, is a new version of "The Zahir," as well as of "The Aleph." Those two magical objects are combined here in the form of a book written in an unknown language, whose pages are infinite in number, so that it is impossible to see again the page and the illustration that one has seen once. The "book of sand" (the name alludes to its infinite nature) is acquired by the protagonist-narrator—like Borges a Buenos Aires native of English origin who used to work in the National Library—from a Bible salesman. The protagonist becomes a prisoner of the undecipherable "Book of Books," constantly counting its pages and dreaming of the book and its magical illustrations, until, realizing that he is losing his mind, but also that burning the book "might likewise prove infinite and suffocate the planet with smoke" (122), he intentionally loses it in the basement of the National Library.

Like most of the volumes contained in the library of Babel, the sand book is written in a language that no one can recognize. It is thus, basically, an empty object, its emptiness alluding to that of the universe, empty of meaning, while the book's infinite nature points to the way that the repetition of human actions (and also of space, as in the "periodic" library) makes the world seem infinite. The book of sand's emptiness precludes its identification with an aleph-like image of the universe capable of stirring one's imagination. Nor is the book truly obsessive, like the aleph's opposite, the zahir, the destroyer of memory. These two conditions are reflected in the relative ease with which the protagonist makes up his mind to get rid of his treasure, and then does so.

I pointed out above that the use of the supernatural seemed to foster the reflection on literature in Borges' stories. The fantastic element pushes away the reality to which the writer would have otherwise to devote at least some attention. He is then free to develop, through the supernatural, the meditation on literature that was the motor of the story. Nothing similar happens in the *ficciones* of the last two books. We find in them one classical fantastic story ("The Meeting") and one horror story, both devoid of any kind of super-text (the philosophical comment that ends "The Meeting" cannot be considered one). The other incursions into the fantastic besides "There Are More Things" featured in *The Book of Sand* are, in the cases of "The Other" and the science-fiction story "Utopia of a Tired Man" excuses to express, rather directly, the same ideology that canonical stories like "Tlön" or "Pierre Menard" suggested in rich, subtle ways. The true fantastic story of *The Book of Sand*, the title story, repeats the basic premise of "The Zahir" and "The Aleph" without developing in full the meaning that the supernatural book could have for its tired owner.

Notes

1. The *ultraísmo* was a Spanish poetic movement that echoed Dadaism in several ways, although it was much less iconoclastic and nihilistic. It relied heavily on the effect of unusual metaphors. Borges lived in Spain precisely during the years when the *ultraísmo* movement was most active, from 1918 to 1921.

2. "This technique or ambition of the ancients has been subjected by Frazer [James George Frazer, author of *The Golden Bough*] to a convenient general law, that of sympathy [chap. 3, "Sympathetic Magic"], which posits an inevitable link between very distant things, be it because their shape is similar—imitative, homeopathic magic—or else because of a previous closeness—contagious magic [the terms are also Frazer's]" (77; my translation).

3. Roberto González Echevarría discusses this essay in the context of magical realism ("Isla a su vuelo fugitiva"), noting that Aristotle's *Poetics* formulated a teleology to which Borges' is analogous, since it also relies on a coherent whole that posits the same structure for all cultures. Ronald Christ (*Narrow Act* 121) also discusses the essay, suggesting that Borges is looking in it for a form capable of replacing psychological motivation and of being applicable to the kind of mythic literature to which he aspires.

4. Borges wrote with Bioy Casares *Seis problemas para don Isidro Parodi* (1942), *Un modelo para la muerte* (1946), *Dos fantasías memorables* (1946), *Los orilleros* (1955), *Crónicas de Bustos Domecq* (1967), etc.

5. In his youth Borges was a great admirer of Dostoevsky, a fact recorded, for instance, in the story "The Other," of *The Book of Sand*. A letter of 1921 says of *Crime and Punishment*: "In my opinion it is the best novel ever written" (*Cartas* 58; my translation).

6. The first part of the book that would eventually be called *Ficciones* appeared in 1942 as *El jardín de senderos que se bifurcan* (the title of its last story, "The Garden of Forking Paths"). The second edition, of 1944, adds six new stories (augmented by three more in the 1956 edition) under the title *Artificios*.

7. See Emir Rodríguez Monegal, "Borges: Una teoría" for a discussion of this lecture. The lecture, "La literatura fantástica," was given in Montevideo in 1949; it was never published. Rodríguez Monegal studies also the preface to Bioy Casares' novel and the essay on magic. Borges' four devices of fantastic literature are also mentioned by James E. Irby in his introduction to Borges' *Labyrinths* (1964, xviii).

8. "Nathaniel Hawthorne" and "De las alegorías a las novelas" (1949). In these essays Borges defends allegory against Croce's charges that it

consists of the needless repetition of a concept which first appears masked by a pseudo-personification of itself (as, in the *Divine Comedy*, Beatrice is supposed to stand for faith), and that it tries to separate content from form by embodying figurative meanings in words designed to carry just their literal meaning. To those arguments, Borges responds by citing Chesterton's argument to the effect that reality is so rich that no single representation of it or of an aspect of it can exhaust it, and that words always embody a plurality of meanings. Borges concludes that the best allegory is the one least able to be reduced to an abstraction. He recognizes, however, that with the triumph of nominalism toward the end of the Middle Ages, the individual replaces the species, and allegory, which had until then been the best way to represent man as a species, is replaced by the novel, which focuses on the individual (see the conclusion of "De las alegorías a las novelas").

9. Maurice Blanchot, "L'infini littéraire"; Gérard Genette, "La littérature selon Borges" and "L'utopie littéraire." Blanchot's essay and Genette's second article are included in *Jorge Luis Borges*, Jaime Alazraki, ed. (Madrid: Taurus, 1976). This collection also includes Emir Rodríguez Monegal's essay "Borges y la *nouvelle critique*," which reviews the use of Borges by the French critics in the 1960s.

10. Since for Derrida the center or origin of the structure of our system of thought is absent, what we have in its place is an interplay of signification, attempts at re-establishing the center; repetitions related to the point of origin, but whose main characteristic is their "differance" (this neologism alludes to difference in space and deferment in time) from the absent center. Writing is then a "productive mechanism" that produces differences; instead of an ultimate meaning for each signifier, we can provide only other signifiers.

11. "Pierre Menard" appeared in *Sur*, No. 56, 1939; "Tlön" in *Sur*, No. 68, 1940. There are two earlier stories, "Hombre de las orillas," of 1933, included as "Hombre de la esquina rosada" in *Historia universal de la infamia* (1936), and "El acercamiento a Almotásim" (see below). (See Alazraki, *La prosa narrativa*, Bibliografía, 408.) In his "An Autobiographical Essay," Borges says that "Pierre Menard" was his first attempt at writing a story, which was followed, since the attempt was successful, by the "more ambitious" "Tlön." He doesn't mention "Hombre de la esquina rosada," and refers to "El acercamiento a Almotásim" as a "forerunner" to "Pierre Menard," since indeed it is a story in the form of a book review, and reviews and poems were all that he had written before the crisis in his life that prompted the writing of "Pierre Menard" (*The Aleph* 243).

12. James E. Irby, "Borges and the Idea of Utopia" (43). Writing about the origin of "Tlön," Irby quotes from a preface by Borges to an anthology

of writings by his mentor Macedonio Fernández in which he explains how he and some friends had planned to write a novel about Macedonio's fantasy of becoming president of Argentina. A group of mad millionaires undertake a campaign to undermine the "people's resistance through the gradual dissemination of 'disturbing inventions' . . . including certain very small and disconcertingly heavy objects (like the cone found . . . toward the end of 'Tlön')'' (41).

13. According to "An Autobiographical Essay" (in *The Aleph*), the story was written in the early part of 1939; it was published in May of 1940 with a "Posdata de 1947" which tells of the intrusion of the invented planet into our world.

14. In a 1933 essay, "La postulación de la realidad," Borges notes that we tend naturally toward imprecision and the simplification of complex states. We perceive reality selectively; living is "an education in forgetfulness" (*Discusión* 61).

15. As stated in "Phaedrus." See in this regard Jacques Derrida's "La pharmacie de Platon" (*La dissémination*).

16. See Ronald Christ's *The Narrow Act*.

17. A similar process occurs in "La busca de Averroes," also of *El aleph* (this story appeared in 1947; "La otra muerte" in 1949, with the title "La redención": see Alazraki, *La prosa narrativa* 409). After describing the Arab philosopher's attempts at understanding the meaning of tragedy and comedy, Borges, in an epilogue to the story, tells us what he tried to accomplish in it and how at the end he felt that the work was making fun of him, that it was absurd to try to imagine Averroes on the basis of a few scholarly references to him. The story is a symbol of the man its writer was as he wrote it; the instant that Borges stops believing in Averroes, he disappears.

18. "El sur" and "El fin" were published in 1953. Borges' next collection of stories, *El informe de Brodie*, appeared in 1970. The tales in it are basically realistic.

19. The wheel that the priest sees when he is united with the divinity is another version of the aleph ("La escritura" appeared in 1949, four years after "The Aleph"). It is made up of "all the things that will be, that are and that were." Tzinacán looks at the wheel and understands everything related to the origin and the fate of the universe, the story of which he sees in the wheel (*El aleph* 120).

20. "The dissemination of objects from Tlön in several countries would have complemented that plan [the one devised by the author of the invented planet's encyclopedia to make that world look not too different from ours]...." A footnote follows: "A problem remaining, naturally, is that of the *matter* of some objects" (*Ficciones* 33).

21. "El acercamiento a Almotásim" appeared originally in *Historia de la eternidad* (1936) and was later incorporated into *Ficciones.*

22. "The student claps his hands once and then a second time and asks for Al-Mu'tasim. A man's voice—the unimaginable voice of Al-Mu'tasim—urges him to enter. The student draws the curtain and moves forward" (39).

23. Examples of this abound: the novel that the narrator and his friend Bioy Casares plan to write in "Tlön"; Hladík's play; the story that the protagonist of "El zahir" is writing; Herbert Quain's novel *April March* and his play *The Secret Mirror.*

24. See my "La nueva metáfora de la creación artística en el cuento de Borges," *Insula* 340 (1975): 5.

25. This year—Borges' thirtieth—is mentioned often in Borges' *ficciones*: Joseph Cartaphilus, "the immortal," died in 1929, as did Beatriz Viterbo, of "El aleph"; it is also the date showing on the coin-zahir. In 1930 a military coup against the elected government in Argentina began a constitutional crisis from which the country has not yet recovered.

26. The English version reads: "as though the knives were coming awake after a long sleep side by side in the cabinet" (*Doctor Brodie* 78).

27. Borges was directly involved in the translation into English of the stories that make up *El informe de Brodie*, as he explains in the Foreword, adding that "the writing and the translation were, except in one case, more or less simultaneous" (7).

28. There was in the 1870s a tough called Juan Moreira. Eduardo Gutiérrez wrote a novel with that title that became very famous (it was made into a play), and Roberto J. Payró another one called *Divertidas aventuras del nieto de Juan Moreira.*

29. Juan Muraña's nephew tells the story to Borges soon after 1930 in order to humiliate him by showing him how he, Emilio Trápani, had a first-hand knowledge of toughs (*malevos*), while Borges, who in his book on Carriego talks a lot about them, didn't know any personally. But Borges begins by recognizing this in the first lines of the story: although he grew up in a tough neighborhood, he was separated from it by the tall fence surrounding the house in whose library he spent most of his time.

30. See his *Supernatural Horror in Literature* (New York, 1945). Talking about "There Are More Things" in the Afterword to *The Book of Sand*, Borges says that he felt he would not have any peace of mind until he "perpetrated a posthumous story by H. P. Lovecraft, a writer whom I have always considered an unconscious parodist of Poe." He then calls the story "lamentable" (*Book of Sand* 124).

31. See Enrique Anderson Imbert's "Un cuento de Borges: 'La casa de Asterión,'" (included in the author's *Crítica interna* [Madrid: Taurus, 1960], and in Alazraki, *Jorge Luis Borges*), which interprets the monster's labyrinth as an

image of the art of Borges—who is perceived as a Minotaur-like figure.

32. In the Afterword Borges says of this story that it is in his "judgement the most honest and melancholy" of the book (124).

33. Seen as a constant repetition of the same events, except for, perhaps, the fact that "Russia is taking over the planet" while "America [notice Borges' obviously deliberate choice of the name employed by Americans to refer to the United States, as their country is generally referred to by Latin Americans and Europeans], tied by the superstition of democracy, hesitates to become an empire[!]" (*Libro de arena* 14).

34. In a book to be called "The Red Hymns" or "The Red Rhythm" (*Libro* 16). While in Spain in 1920 Borges wrote a book "titled either *The Red Psalms* or *The Red Rhythms*. It was a collection of poems—perhaps some twenty in all—in free verse and in praise of the Russian Revolution, the brotherhood of man, and pacifism. Three or four of them found their way into magazines—'Bolshevik Epic,' 'Trenches,' 'Russia.' This book I destroyed on the eve of our departure" (*The Aleph* 223). "Russia" was included in *Indice de la nueva poesía americana*, prol. by Alberto Hidalgo, Vicente Huidobro, and Jorge Luis Borges (Buenos Aires: Sociedad de Publicaciones El Inca, 1926). It is an *ultraísta* poem: "La trinchera avanzada es en la estepa un barco al abordaje . . . Bajo banderas de silencio pasa la muchedumbre . . . El mar vendrá nadando a esos ejércitos / Que envolverán sus tonos / En todas las praderas del naciente . . . Bayonetas / Que llevan en la punta las mañanas."

Chapter Three

Cortázar's Approach to the Fantastic

The other internationally renowned Argentinean writer, Julio Cortázar, is also considered to be a master of the fantastic. Cortázar's fantastic stories are closer to the canons of the genre than are Borges', or at least they appear to be so at first glance.

Of the eight texts that make up Cortázar's first book of short stories, *Bestiario* (1951), six fall comfortably within the boundaries of the fantastic. The other two, "Omnibus" and "Circe," do not include the supernatural in any way, but both contain sufficient extraordinary elements (in "Omnibus," two bus passengers are physically threatened by their fellow passengers for not, like themselves, carrying flowers, since the bus's destination is the cemetery; in "Circe," a neurotic young woman makes cockroach-stuffed candies for her boyfriends) to allow them to be categorized as uncanny. According to Todorov's definition, in that borderline genre an explanation of the apparently unnatural element, no matter how unconvincing it might be, is offered at the end.

Contrary to what happens in Borges' stories, where characterization plays a minimal role, all the *Bestiario* narratives pay careful attention to the thoughts of the characters, and in some cases to their psychological development as well. The same can be said of most of Cortázar's fiction, which is particularly effective in drawing realistic, believable portraits. Thus, the supernatural makes its appearance in almost all of Cortázar's fantastic stories within a totally familiar world, as happens also in Kafka's

61

narratives. The convincing psychological portraits found in *Bestiario* make a particularly sharp contrast with the supernatural or wholly inexplicable event with which those characters come into contact, the only element of the story that escapes verisimilitude.

In "Cefalea," a narrator who refers to him/herself in the plural and then switches genders in the course of her/his account,[1] describes the task of caring for animals of an unidentified and also variable specie, the man-cuspias, whose moods, as well as the overwhelming demands that their care imposes, have an increasingly detrimental effect on the physical and mental health of their keepers. All of this is explained in detail in a scientific manual. What at first seems like a description of the care of an exotic mammal and of how exhausted that work leaves the narrator and her/his companion, ends up being, basically, the description of a mental state (whose symptoms begin to be introduced on the second page under a scientific guise). Consequently, the mancuspias appear to exist only in that manual's (but is this a real text?) description of how their behavior affects their keepers, while the house where the action seems to be taking place is, as the narrator says, "our head."[2]

Since we know even less—nothing, in fact—about the personality and background of the human protagonists of this story or the nature of their charge, than we know about the characters in a novel by Kafka, the task of translating them, their work, and the mancuspias into appropriate concepts becomes even more difficult than is the same task in relation to the various elements of a Kafka story. It seems correct to assume that those strange animals, sometimes bird-like, sometimes furry, sometimes slippery like seals, stand for our obsessions. But since this is all that can be said with any degree of certainty of the mancuspias, it is best to concentrate on the narrative itself in order to analyze its technique, or the feelings and thoughts that it stirs in us. And this is actually what most critics have done.

In fact, the rhetoric of the narrative works, in this as well as in other *Bestiario* stories, against any kind of extratextual interpretation, due to the characterization and the detailed description of reality. While most allegorical texts draw a sketchy picture of reality so that their message can be conveyed more efficiently or with minimum interference from realistic detail and anecdote, Cortázar's *Bestiario* stories tend to lock us into the world they depict by making it thoroughly lifelike. Yet the very unreality of the narrated events constantly urges the reader to dismiss that reality as a value in itself and look for what it must be serving as a vehicle for.

"Cefalea" does not provoke surprise at the intrusion of the supernatural of the sort that characterizes the classical fantastic. This is due to the fact that the mysterious subjects of the story slowly develop into supernatural beings before our eyes. At the same time, the story depends for its effect on suspense and eventually even fear. At the end the mancuspias have escaped and surround the house where their by now exhausted ex-keepers have been left alone without light or food. Our uncertainty as to the nature of these animals, which grows as they grow increasingly unreal, turns into doubt by the time the story is finished, regarding the truthfulness of the narrator's account: has she/he dreamt this; is he/she mad?

"House Taken Over" also relies to some degree on the fear and suspense typical of a certain type of fantastic story. Here a man and his sister, both unmarried and greatly devoted to each other, witness as their big, comfortable Buenos Aires house is taken over in two stages by strangers. When these strangers reach the section of the house where the brother and sister have confined themselves, the two flee it forever. "House," *Bestiario*'s opening story and one of Cortázar's best known,[3] has been interpreted since its publication as alluding to "the dark presences that we create" and that take hold of us (as it was described on the back cover of the original edition of *Bestiario*). More recently, it has been read as an allegory in which the house's owners stand for the Argentinean bourgeoisie (they are financially very well off thanks to the income they receive from the lands they own; the house was built by their grandparents), and their predicament and their response to it, for the way the upper classes felt when they were suddenly threatened by the masses whose power the Peronista movement had unleashed.[4] This reading can be interpreted, in turn, as leading to either of two opposite conclusions from the perspective of the author. In one, Cortázar may be seen as supporting the reasons for the brother and sister's flight in his own departure from Argentina, never to return to it permanently, the same year that *Bestiario* was published.[5] In the other interpretation, their habits, exclusive dependence on each other, and fears about losing their property are meant to be seen as ironic, and their eviction as well deserved. This last interpretation points toward Cortázar's political commitment of later years.

But "House" calls also—as does "Cefalea" even more pointedly, due to the forcefulness and the centrality of its protagonist-narrator—for an interpretation of the type that has been applied to *The Turn of the Screw*, which questions the truthfulness of the account of the events by pointing to the unreliability of the narrator. The brother and sister live in total isolation; they receive no visitors and almost never go out. (The man does leave the house on Saturdays, like a white-collar worker who has only the weekends free, to buy wool for his sister's knitting and to do some unsuccessful bookstore browsing in search of novelties in French literature, which confirms his belief that "since 1939 nothing worthwhile reaches Argentina" [*Bestiario* 11].) But what is even more extraordinary, especially for members of the Latin American bourgeoisie, which this couple seem to be, is that, in spite of their wealth (when they leave the house the man realizes that he has forgotten to take with him fifteen thousand pesos—a rather substantial sum at the time—that he had in a wardrobe), they do not have a single servant, so that they have to do all the cooking and clean the big house by themselves. This suggests that we read the story as the hallucination of a madman who is perhaps writing from an insane asylum, and whose real social circumstances, which are actually unconsciously reflected in his narrative, are very different from those he imagines for himself; someone in fact, like the protagonist of the play "The Enemies," by the writer Hladík of Borges' "The Secret Miracle," who is actually dreaming the aristocratically-clad drama that the playwright presents at first as the straight version of real events.[6]

It could be argued, at the same time, that casting doubt on the testimony of the narrator on the grounds just summarized constitutes a critical reading totally independent of authorial intentions. It is possible, and perhaps even likely if one considers the whole of *Bestiario* in the context of Cortázar's subsequent evolution, that he might have paid no attention whatsoever to the *real* background and environment of the protagonists of "House" while giving expression to the strange, obsessive forces that roam through the stories of that collection.[7]

There is not in "House," at any rate, a presentation of the narrator and of the background of his story of the sort that in *The Turn of the Screw* actually calls for rejecting the reality of the ghosts. Any doubts as to the veracity of the protagonist-narrator's account in "House" have thus to be developed outside the narrative itself. Meanwhile, the hesitation as to the nature of the house's intruders, which is stirred by the suddenness of their appearance, is maintained after the close of the story, in the tradition of the purest examples of the fantastic genre. It should be noted also that the intrusion of the uncanny (the intruders, although their being in the house could be accounted for only through supernatural causes, appear to be human beings), and thus our initial hesitation, follows here a much more "classical" pattern than that of "Cefalea," whose strange animals develop into supernatural beings little by little.

"Letter to a Young Lady in Paris" consists of an account by the letter's author, the protagonist of the story, of how, since his arrival in the addressee's beautifully furnished apartment, his habit of vomiting a bunny—and then keeping it for a short while—every four or five weeks, has grown worse, resulting in an overproduction of those cute animals, which now add up to eleven. Not knowing what to do any more about an until now relatively controllable peculiarity that has turned into an intolerable disease, the narrator commits suicide.

As in both "House" and "Cefalea," the absence of an omniscient narrator to testify to the presence of the dead bunnies (the protagonist kills them too) entitles the reader to interpret the contents of the letter as the hallucination of a schizophrenic. And as in the other two stories, allegorical interpretations are easily admissible. The little bunnies so appealing to children could represent an infantile (representative of what the protagonist's inner self is really like) refuge from the anxieties of modern life. These anxieties are felt in a particularly acute way by the narrator, a professional translator (as Cortázar once was), without a family or a permanent domicile (he changes houses every few months). He keeps his ängst under control through the ritualized vomiting of bunnies until it is aggravated by the contrast between the tidiness and refined elegance of the apartment that he has sublet and his own insecurity. The order with which he then tries to replace his old one (the expelling of a rabbit once a month), i.e., keeping the bunnies hidden during the day and feeding and playing with them at night, proves to be unsatisfactory, as the continuing production of bunnies demonstrates.

Here too, as in "House," two opposite political interpretations of the story are possible. The protagonist's reaction to his new surroundings might constitute a critique of bourgeois culture as exemplified by the dwelling and the habits of the young lady now traveling in France. But it could also be a criticism of the masses that reproduce themselves like rabbits, threatening with destruction our intellectual—or if one wishes, bourgeois—order.

While in "Cefalea" it was difficult to fix allegorical readings to the story, in the latter two stories acceptable allegorical interpretations come easily to mind. In "Letter," furthermore, the allegorical interpretation or meta-text, which rests, in turn, on a psychological explanation of the protagonist-narrator's behavior, seems the only possible one, due to the utter impossibility of the central event (the vomiting of bunnies). Mancuspias and house invaders can be considered too to be inventions of mentally ill narrators; but they can be explained rationally as distortions of real animals or people, or even—in the case of the latter—as ghosts. The very preposterousness of those bunnies, on the other hand, demands that we read them as symbolic. And in addition their "father" 's narrative casts

very serious doubts on his own mental stability: he mentions how they cry
and yell and place themselves in a circle in order to adore him, and how
he punishes one bunny by placing it standing against the wall for hours
(*Bestiario* 30, 32–33).

The stories examined so far belong ostensibly within the "fantastic
marvelous" (the supernatural accepted). But if, ignoring what the texts
claim, we pay due attention to the unreliability of the narrators, our doubts
regarding the three supernatural subjects intensify in the direction of
outright rejection of them, while allegorical explanations seem much more
satisfactory for explaining the stories. Yet the solid, lifelike reality surrounding mancuspias, house invaders, and even bunnies makes casting
these texts into firm, univocal allegories very difficult if not altogether
impossible, even in the case of "Letter," whose higher degree of impossibility presses for an allegorical reading.

"The Gates of Heaven" has a first-person narrator too, but of a very
different type from those in the preceding stories. Marcelo Hardoy is a
sophisticated observer, a lawyer with literary inclinations who takes a
distinctly detached view of the events he is narrating, and who constantly
makes mental notes on the habits of his subjects (he refers to the *fichas*,
or index cards, that he keeps or is planning to write [127, 128]), in this
case a couple of lower class origin, whom he has befriended while representing them in a lawsuit. Soon after the wife, Celina, dies of tuberculosis,
the narrator takes the widower, Mauro, in order to help distract him from
his sorrow, to a cheap dance hall, similar to the ones where Celina worked
as a dancer before meeting Mauro. And there, emerging from the clouds
of heavy cigarette smoke, lost in the pleasure of dancing, both men see
Celina—Celina in paradise, the way she would have felt as a dancer had
it not been for the work and the customers; Celina finally happy in her
"conquered heaven" (138), enjoying her reward for having been a good,
loving wife in an environment (that of Mauro, a shopkeeper) that she
didn't love. Celina's husband tries to brush away the vision by asking his
friend: "Did you notice how much she [the woman both saw] resembled
her?" (ibid.); but then he runs after her all the same, trying to find again
"the gates of heaven."

The doubt concerning the supernatural, which in the preceding stories
had to be developed by the reader outside the text itself, is here introduced
within it, at its very end. This immediately follows the intrusion of the
supernatural, also at the end of the story, which until that point seems
aimed solely at painting a social and psychological portrait. The careful
drawing of that picture would by itself suffice to make allegorical interpre-

tations seem remote. But the narrator himself eliminates that possibility when he explains fully, also in realistic, psychological terms, the meaning of the dead woman's presence at the "Santa Fe Palace." We may or may not believe him regarding the apparition—one that is not frightening per se—which he is absolutely certain of having seen; his interpretation of it, meanwhile, sounds entirely satisfactory and stays within the parameters of the social picture that the story so masterfully paints.

The denial of the occurrence of the supernatural by the only other witness lends force to the reader's doubt regarding the possibility of the supernatural. He may follow Mauro in dismissing the apparition. Yet since the narrator of this story seems to be just the opposite of the neurotic, unreliable narrators of "House," "Letter," and "Cefalea" (although it could be argued that his literary interests have influenced in the direction of the fantastic his perception of the incident), and since the deceased woman's husband is so impressed also by the "resemblance" between Celina and the dancer they both saw that he cannot help running after her, the impossible ends up making a much stronger claim for acceptance in this story than in any of the other *Bestiario* stories except "The Distances."

"The Distances" ("Lejana": "far away," in the original) features an outside narrator who, in the three paragraphs that make up the last segment of the story tells us its "real" denouement. The protagonist, a rich Argentinean young lady writes in her diary (the main narrative is in the form of diary fragments) about how she is being haunted first in her dreams and then also when seemingly awake by the presence of a poor and physically abused Budapest woman. Alina Reyes goes to that city for her honeymoon, with the intention of meeting her pursuer and ridding herself of the obsession that she represents (she thinks of herself as an always victorious queen, as evidenced by her surname, Reyes, which means kings). But what happens is, naturally, the opposite. Alina, explains the narrator, meets her double and embraces her; they switch bodies, and the new Alina, now shivering with cold, the snow entering her broken shoes, watches herself walking away in all her radiant beauty and elegance.

Our doubts concerning the reality of the strange woman's visitations to the protagonist as recorded in her diary are closed off by the epilogue, which confirms the occurrence of the supernatural. And the outside narrator further strengthens his testimony's authenticity by telling us that the false Alina divorced her husband only two months after the trip to Buda-pest, something which might be the natural consequence, on the one hand, of her being actually a different person from the one she pretends to be, or on the other, of the fact that Alina had married exclusively in order to make the trip possible. (Notice the parallel between the names of Buenos Aires and Buda-Pest, as well as how the women meet in the exact middle of the bridge connecting the two halves of the Hungarian capital.)

This story clearly implies a search for another reality, and more to the point, for a passage to it through a breach in the day-to-day reality. That search characterizes Cortázar's subsequent work. Because it tells its story—that of the pursuit by and then the meeting with one's double—in a straightforward manner, "The Distances" suggests more definitely than does any other *Bestiario* story that, notwithstanding its richness as far as action and psychological development, we read it as an allegory of the search for the authentic self.[8] (The story could be read also, from a political perspective, as a critique of the privileged, who end up here, in the person of the protagonist, being abruptly dispossessed of their riches.) Yet "The Distances" is a full-fledged fantastic story in which the supernatural develops into a physical presence that is eventually accepted by the narrator as being real.

Undoubtedly the most original of all the stories included in *Bestiario* is the title story. "Bestiary"'s narrator is external, but of the type that Todorov defines as being "on a basis of equality with the *he* of the hero; both are informed in the same way as to the development of the action" (*Poetics* 27). I notice only one intervention of the traditional outside narrator: "She wasn't old enough to be able to understand ..." (146). This is the type of narrator who favors the *style indirect libre* perfected by Flaubert.

The protagonist of the story is a girl, probably around ten years old, who is invited to the country estate of some relatives (an aunt and two uncles?) to spend the summer so that the son of one of the two gentlemen, a boy slightly younger than she, will have a playmate. That many of the relationships between the characters are never clarified is an effect of the narrator's closeness to the viewpoint of the protagonist, who does not feel the need to explain what she knows very well. In the very first page of the story, as the girl's mother and another woman, probably an aunt, discuss the invitation, the existence of a tiger living on the estate is mentioned, though they state at the same time that "after all, they are very careful about that aspect" (*Bestiario* 139). The technique here is the same as that employed in "Letter," where the existence of the bunnies is introduced in a matter-of-fact fashion in the second line of the narrative.

The tiger—who moves, under close watch or directed by guards, from one part of the garden to another, and even between some of the rooms of the house as wild beasts move between the various sections of their cages in zoos and circuses—is accepted by Isabel, the protagonist, as something almost normal, a presence whose movements are well controlled and to whom everyone in the household is accustomed. Her mother, in fact, warned her not to ask any questions regarding the tiger; and Rema, the lady of the house, prevents Isabel, without saying anything explicitly, from making such a faux pas. Isabel knows, however, that "the important reasons are still missing" (156). But what really begins to worry her very soon is Rema's growing sadness as she tries to fend off "el Nene"'s (her brother?) sexual advances. Isabel catches Nene grabbing Rema's fingertips as if by accident. She realizes when Nene slaps Nino's face that the reason why he does so is not because his nephew broke a window (Nino takes the blame for what Isabel actually did), but out of jealousy because Rema reciprocates the boy's affection for her. Isabel also witnesses Nene's surprise and angry trembling when, at Rema's imploring request, she takes to his room the lemonade that he had ordered her to ask Rema to bring to him. She also overhears Nino's father calling Nene (his brother, most likely)[9] a bastard after listening to Rema's explanation of why she is crying.

Then one day after the family finishes eating lunch, Isabel—whose reports on the whereabouts of the tiger, supposedly coming always from the estate's overseer, are by now as trusted as Nino's—deliberately gives the wrong information as to where the tiger is. And thus Nene, whom the girl hates because of the way he makes Rema suffer, certain that the beast is in his study, as Isabel has said, goes into the library, where the tiger actually is at the moment, and is killed by it. The last scene of the story pictures Isabel crying violently, her head buried in Rema's lap, and the latter comforting the girl and whispering something in her ear, "stammering as if out of gratitude, of a nameless consent" (165).

How is one to interpret this short novella, so effective that it would be sufficient to make the reputation of any writer? The realism of the psychological portraits of the protagonist and the other characters as seen through her eyes does not really work in "Bestiary" against developing an allegorical reading, as it does in "Gates," where the ghost's presence is explained in logical terms. The tiger could very well represent the instincts, the animal side of the self, which ends up killing him who lets himself be dominated by the beast inside him (notice how Nene "always knows" where the tiger is, although Isabel avoids asking him). It could also stand for the forbidden, for that which is to be avoided at all costs. The wild animal is released so that it can fulfill its mission, by the only innocent member of the household besides Nino; and in doing this, she loses her innocence. (Nino, being younger than the protagonist, is further away from the possibility of losing his innocence.)[10] It is highly unusual, however, for an allegorical text—assuming that the preceding interpretation is valid—to be as respectful of psychological verisimilitude as this one is. In fact, "Bestiario" is a masterpiece of a subgenre of psychological fiction which features children as protagonists, and in which Cortázar has produced two other masterpieces, "The Poisons" and "End of the Game," neither of which contains fantastic elements.

Since the omniscient narrator functions in "Bestiario" to confirm the protagonist's account of the events, we have no basis for rejecting or even doubting this account by interpreting it as the creation of a neurotic mind. The impossible, that an untamed tiger would live on an estate almost as if it was just another member of the household, must be accepted. From that point of view the story belongs within the impossible accepted category of the fantastic. The fantastic element is here, however, of a particularly concrete nature, much more so than other fantastic intruders in the *Bestiario* stories, some of which remain unseen ("House Taken Over"), or are by definition elusive (the mancuspias, or, for different reasons, Alina Reyes' double). The bunnies of "Letter" are, of course, much more impossible than the tiger, on account of the way they come into the world; but as I argued above, there are clues in that story that definitely suggest that we question their very existence. In "Bestiario," on the other hand, the tiger that dominates the narrative from the very beginning with its enigmatic presence is seen and dealt with by all the characters. The doubt regarding the impossible which is represented by the protagonist's withheld questions about the tiger's presence in the midst of her uncles' (?) home is never addressed in the story, but instead, forcefully ignored. Consequently, the narrative is able to devote its full attention to the psychological interplay of the characters, something which, in turn, calls for rejecting the very notion that is central to the story: the existence of the tiger.

An allegorical reading of "Bestiary" seems to be the only possible solution to the basic impossibility of its central element, the tiger in the house. Notice, by the way, that contrary to what happens in medieval and Renaissance examples of the genre, where the allegorical reading rests on many characters and incidents, in this case it is located in only one element of the story, from which it extends to cover all or most of the story's connotations. In this regard, the specificity of the tiger as the allegorical vehicle is even more marked than that of the bunnies or of the house invaders. Meanwhile, everything in the organization of the narrative, which unfolds as a story about growing up, conspires against our seeing it as allegorical at all.

"Bestiary" brings to a culmination that is also a dead end of sorts the oppositional nature of the relationship between psychological realism and the supernatural that governs the development of plots in the fantastic genre, and that characterizes the stories of *Bestiario*. The fantastic element it introduces is so concrete (to the point of being able to kill someone) that it cannot easily be integrated with the thrust of the story as can other, ghostlike supernatural occurrences ("Gates," "The Distances"). Its independence from the story in which it exists leaves us no other alternative than to search for an extratextual, i.e., allegorical interpretation of it. But this path, the one that we must eventually follow in so many fantastic narratives, is in turn obstructed once again by the psychological verisimilitude of the description.

In the final account, the explanation of and the only way out of this collision of contradictory possibilities for reading the story is one that applies to the whole of *Bestiario*. The stories in this book, including the two non-fantastic ones ("Omnibus" and "Circe") are, rather than allegories, expressions of the writer's absorbing preoccupation with establishing a passage between two levels of consciousness, the quotidian and the imaginary. At the end of "The Gates of Heaven," when Mauro tries to dismiss Celina's appearance as being merely a case of resemblance between two women, the narrator comments that his friend is already "on this side, the poor guy is on this side and could not believe in what we both had known" (138). In "Bestiary," the book's closing story, the characters seem constantly to move between those two sides. The passage sought by the author from one to the other has been opened and then kept open for anyone who dares to pass through it by the fantasy of the child whose independence from the laws of reason allows her to walk freely from reality into the world of the imagination. Of course, all fantastic stories are about a communication between two worlds, but Cortázar's are directly involved with the enactment of that communication, with portraying how it takes place.

In his next two books of stories, *End of the Game* (1956) and *The Secret Weapons* (1959), Cortázar deals very often with the passage between reality and the world of the imagination. That passage, or more accurately, what makes that passage possible, is (since it escapes the laws of nature) supernatural. Thus it brings into the realm of the fantastic those stories in which it *takes place* more or less clearly—but not so those other stories in which it is merely sought or suggested as the background for a communication that its presence enhances. We will examine the stories that fall within the first category, together with those that include the supernatural but in which the contact between the real and the unreal does not necessarily take the form of a passage. Cortázar's newer stories insist on the reality of the impossible in different ways than did the more classically fantastic stories of *Bestiario*, provoking our hesitation by the forcefulness with which a decidedly supernatural event, presence, or being is inscribed in them within a realistic setting. The new stories, however, are not any less attentive to realistic detail and psychological characterization than the ones that make up the 1951 collection.

In the 1970 edition in three volumes of Cortázar's collected stories, *Los relatos*, the author divides them into "Rites," "Games," and "Passages." (A 1968 Spanish edition of *Final del juego* and *Las armas secretas* had been titled *Ceremonias*.) "Bestiary," "Letter to a Young Lady in Paris," "The Night Face Up," "A Story with a Water Background," "The Idol of the Cyclades," "Omnibus," "The Menades," "Circe," "Severo's Phases," "Letters from Mamma," and "Manuscript Found in a Pocket" are classified as "rites." The edition includes two other "rites" not previously collected: "With Authentic Pride" and "The Trip." "Games" includes "Continuity of Parks," "The Condemned Door," "Do Not Blame Anyone," "The River," "Instructions for John Howell," "Cefalea," "Summer," "All Fires the Fire," "The Southern Thruway," and also some stories not previously collected: "The Season of the Hand" and "Sylvia." Finally, "Passages" includes "House Taken Over," "Axolotl," "The Distances," "A Yellow Flower," "The Gates of Heaven," "The Secret Weapons," "Throat of a Black Kitten," "The Island at Noon," and "The Other Heaven." This volume includes a new story: "The Deepest Caress."[11]

A close look at these stories suggests that the categories used by their author to arrange them are interchangeable. They can in fact be subsumed into the general category of "passages," since "rites" and "games" seem to be but preparations for the "passage" which is reserved as a category for only a few stories, but which actually takes place in many others.

Three stories from *End of the Game* seem connected by the evocation of the world of dreams, or, put another way, they are related through their oneiric treatment of the supernatural passage. In "Continuity of Parks" a man who is reading a novel about a crime becomes the victim of that same crime.[12] In "The River" the protagonist talks mentally to his lover, who, like so often in the course of their relationship, had left the room during a quarrel threatening to throw herself in the river, but who is now back. Excited by the woman's presence, the protagonist (who is also the narrator) makes love to her, only to discover that he is next to a puddle of water, since the woman has actually drowned.[13] In "A Story with a Water Backgound" a first-person narrator tells a friend of a dream he has had many times in which he sees a drowned man floating toward him in the river. When he told the dream to another friend (an estranged lover whom he perhaps killed by pushing him into the river?), the latter revealed that the protagonist had stolen that dream from him, and that he had wanted that very place by the river where they were standing. At that precise moment the narrator recognizes the face of the drowned man as his own. He feels now that the man he killed is emerging from the water in order to fetch him.

In all of these stories the impossible element has a dreamlike quality that acts against the full development of the fantastic effect. This applies even to "The River," in which we have a proof—the soaking bed—of the narrator's encounter with the drowned woman. As we have seen again and again, the fantastic effect is based on the impact of the intrusion of the uncanny or the supernatural into the world of everyday reality. In the *End of the Game* stories described above we seem instead to be dealing with the communication between the merely rational, and higher, more fulfilling levels of consciousness. The latter is what functions in these narratives as the fantastic. And it does so, except in "The River," without including the actual occurrence of the supernatural ("Continuity" could, after all, be explained as an extraordinary coincidence between literature and reality; the protagonist of "A Story with a Water Background" could simply be imagining his own death as punishment for a crime that he may have committed.) In other words, at least two of those stories are not about the appearance of the supernatural within normal reality, but about the mind transcending reality, which remains unaffected by that process; thus their oneiric tone.

The affirmation made by these stories that a passage out of ordinary reality is possible precludes any kind of uncertainty as to the appearance of the impossible in them. And it also precludes allegorical readings. The stories are, notwithstanding their connection with the world of dreams and the supernatural, capable of explanation without going outside of the text.

"Do Not Blame Anyone" does not have the oneiric quality of the preceding stories. In this story, a man who is putting on a pullover sweater with a great deal of difficulty because of the apparent refusal of one of his hands to perform the motions that he wants it to, finds himself threatened by that same hand. Fleeing from its dark menace, he falls out an open window to his death. The extraordinary yet very concrete events that take place in this fantastic story point not so much to any kind of extrasensory communication as to a vicious and in the end tragic split within the protagonist. This suggests a connection with existentialist philosophy. As illustrated by some of Sartre's best known works of fiction, existentialism explored man's awareness of his personality's various sides as so many concrete unities, with the purpose of achieving a fully conscious existence. The deliberate defamiliarization of the mechanism that allows us to remain unaware of the different elements that make up our consciousness leads to the revelation of reality as being absurd. And absurdity plays, of course, an important role in "Do Not Blame Anyone."

"A Yellow Flower" seems fantastic in a more traditional way. A man discovers little by little that a young boy whom he has met by chance on a bus is a reincarnation of himself who, through an error in time's mechanism, was born before he himself had died. And so he kills the boy in order to prevent the repetition of his own empty existence. Being the first "mortal" human being fills the protagonist with happiness until the day when he realizes that he will never again be able to enjoy, through the person in whom he was supposed to be reincarnated, the beauty of the simple yellow flower of the title. He then begins to look desperately for another version of himself. The story is told by an outside narrator who relates what a drunkard told him and others at a bistro. The owner's and the other customers' laughter at the man's account of our immortality serves as the vehicle for the hesitation typical of the fantastic. The narrator, however, is convinced of the truth of what he has heard—which is, after all, but a dramatic account of the idea of reincarnation.

This story features a reversal of the process described by Borges in "The Immortal," which begins as a search for immortality and ends as a search for mortality. "A Yellow Flower" 's focus on humble objects and people contrasts with Borges' immortal's reliance for references on famous characters and actions. To the notion of a passage between different realms this story adds that of a passage between different times, as we will see also in others of Cortázar's stories.

"Axolotl," "The Night Face Up," and "The Idol of the Cyclades," also from End of the Game, are paradigmatic "passage" stories. While "Axolotl" is narrated in the first person, the other two are told by outside narrators; in the case of "Night," a narrator of the close-by type that we encountered in "Bestiary." In "Axolotl" the narrator describes his own transformation into an axolotl after becoming fascinated with that rare species of salamander. "Night" tells how a young man lying on his back in a hospital bed while recovering from a motorcycle accident is transformed into a warrior[14] of pre-Columbian Mexico about to be sacrificed to the Aztec gods, so that as he dies in the temple, it is the accident and the hospital that seem to be a dream. The last story narrates the effect that a pre-classical Greek idol has on the two men who have found it and who revive in their own persons the original meaning of the statuette as the object of a bloody rite.

None of these passages through matter and time is fantastic in the same sense as that in "The Gates of Heaven." Both "Axolotl" and "Idol" could ultimately be explained as illustrations of the power of suggestion (or self-suggestion, especially in the case of "Axolotl"). "Night" belongs, as does "The Secret Weapons," which we will discuss shortly, in the gray area of extrasensory perception and communication among spirits, about which so much has been written but so little concluded. Of course, these types of contacts are by nature supernatural, but many insist, at the same time, on explaining them according to natural laws. From the point of view of Todorov's categories for the fantastic, "Idol" and "Night" fall within the fantastic-uncanny since there is in them a definite wish to make the impossible appear as an acceptable phenomenon, i.e., to explain it. "Axolotl," on the other hand, due to the virtual impossibility of the transformation that it portrays, presents us with no other alternative to simply dismissing the axolotl's testimony as the delusion of a madman than to accept the supernatural as such.

Contrary to the stories discussed previously, in these three the actual occurrence of some sort of supernatural communication is carefully developed in the narrative in a manner closely resembling that of the classical fantastic, although without making direct use of the characteristic uncertainty. The extraordinary, impossible, or almost impossible event is presented as having actually taken place rather than as an uncanny coincidence, as something that may occur or that happened in a dream, or, as in the case of "A Yellow Flower," as a character's testimony, apparently accepted but nonetheless, because it is distanced from the reader by being retold by a narrator who heard the original testimony, also susceptible to outright rejection (the "mortal" could be an unusually articulate drunkard). (In "The River" the supernatural appears as a fact, but it lacks the weight, due to the story's oneiric quality as well as to its shortness, that the supernatural communication has in "Night," "Idol," and "Axolotl.")

It seems clear, at the same time, that the uncanny or the supernatural, whether explained, accepted, or left undecided (as in "Flower") is not the real object of Cortázar's interest. He is concerned instead with the possibilities it opens up for that passage between the quotidian and the imaginary that he wishes to grab and hold open even if only for a fraction of a second.

In "Axolotl" and "Idol" that passage is actively sought by the protagonist, while in "Night" the young man puts up an anguished struggle against it as he tries to wake up into the hospital but finds himself more and more often waking up on "the other side": "He was inside the sacred time, on the other side of where the hunters were" (*Ceremonies* 135). This story has an obvious link with "The Distances," another instance of extrasensory communication, except that in the latter story the passage is actively pursued by both women until they find the door leading to it. Another difference is that in "Night" the passage takes place independently of the protagonist's will, during those moments when he has lost consciousness due to the motorcycle accident.[15] The consequences of the transit through that passage are tragic in two of the three stories under discussion, and unhappy in "Axolotl." Here the narrator, once he is fully on the axolotl's side of the aquarium, first feels like a prisoner inside the body of that tiny animal, and later reflects that all communication between him and the man he used to be has ended with his transformation into the object of his obsession. All he can hope for now is that the man whom he used to be, thinking that he is writing a fantastic story, will write about "all this" (130). His wish to enter into the existence of these practically motionless, seemingly prehistoric larvae who appeared to the narrator to spend all their time watching and thinking, seems akin to the death wish explored by Freud.[16]

The subject of "Idol" is the actual search for the passage. The protagonist, a River Plate native living in Paris—the first in a long series of expatriate Latin Americans, and more specifically Argentineans, in Cortázar's works—applies himself for a long time to reproducing the small statue that he and his French friend, Morand, had found in Greece two summers before. He does this in order to reach an identification "with the [statue's] original structure, through a superimposition that would be more than just that, because at that point there won't be a duality any longer, but a fusion" (64). Somoza, the Latin American, reaches that identification through his physical contact with the statuette, which he reproduces again and again. By the end of the story, he has achieved, without being a sculptor (he is an archeologist), an almost exact replica of the original.

The reader of Latin American literature cannot but think at this point of Pierre Menard and his reproduction of the *Quixote* achieved also through repeated attempts at reproducing its text. But while Menard wishes with his "writing" of *Don Quixote* to obliterate it as the work of an individual genius, Somoza wants to become the "author" of the statue in order to understand what it meant to the primitive people of a still matriarchal Greece who worshiped it; he wants to fuse himself with the idol. Menard wants to prove that all intellectuals are capable of thinking all the thoughts and writing all the books; Somoza wants to show that an intellectual can identify with the spirit that created the idol.

In order to complete his union with the goddess represented by the statue Somoza has to perform a human sacrifice. But the person that he chooses to sacrifice, Morand, the typically logical Frenchman, not only repels his friend's attack, but kills him with the stone hatchet that Somoza himself was brandishing. Then, after smearing the idol with the blood of the man he has killed, he undresses and prepares to sacrifice his wife, whom he had asked, without knowing why, to join him and Somoza that afternoon.

As in "The Night Face Up," with which this story shares notable affinities, the passage leads to a world of primitive beliefs. The feeling of being prisoner to those beliefs that causes the growing terror of "Night"'s protagonist is, in "Idol," what first ignites Somoza's active search for those beliefs, and then, allows him, having opened the door to the collective unconscious, to physically involve someone else who had seemed thoroughly rooted in the Western rational tradition in a primitive "rite"— which is how the story is categorized in *Los relatos*.

Everything in Cortázar's previous work—*Bestiario*, the play *The Kings*, the novel *The Winners*—as well as in the texts contemporary with the stories that we have been examining and those that follow them points to the search for a passage to another realm of consciousness. This, once the communication with it is established, can liberate the full power of the imagination, allowing it to jump over the barriers posed by time and space, and even to revive our most ancient selves (as happens in "Axolotl," "Night," and "Idol"). Through the evocation and eventual description—in the last three stories mentioned—of that passage, Cortázar moves away from the fantastic, to which he was closer in his first book. At that time the idea of such a passage was not the central concern of the writing, but only a possibility that was introduced in the critical interpretation of the stories to explain the intrusion of the supernatural into a solidly realistic world whose uncertainty was made apparent by that intrusion.

In Cortázar's later stories, as he became increasingly preoccupied with the notion of crossing to "the other side," the passage would cease to appear as something supernatural or even uncanny, and as such capable of disrupting reality. It would change from a mere intuition into a belief to be pursued, no longer in opposition to the world as routinely perceived, but within it, in order to make us aware of what we normally ignore. As the vision sought by Cortázar gains in strength and definition, the passage that leads to it seems larger and, consequently, less uncertain; in fact, hardly uncertain at all. This is why the new stories strike the reader as being less fantastic than those in *Bestiario*, and tend in fact to fall outside the genre altogether. Absent from them is any kind of hesitation regarding the presence of the supernatural.

In *Bestiario*, the notion of a passage is suggested more or less explicitly in only one of the stories (''The Gates of Heaven''), and left in the rest to be intuited from the superposition of fantastic and realistic worlds. It is never developed there, as it would be later in ''Flower,'' ''Idol,'' and ''Axolotl'' as a result of Cortázar's growing commitment to positing an actual communication between the real world and that of extra-sensory perceptions, the reality of neither of which is questioned. The contact between those two worlds is always very brief in the *Bestiario* stories, whether it happens only once or several times in the course of the narrative. Actually, only in two of the stories from the 1951 book, the ones that employ an outside narrator (''Bestiary'' and ''The Distances''), is there a ''proof'' rather than merely a suggestion of that contact having taken place; and even in those texts there seems to be an empty space between the real and the fantastic in which we can exercise our doubt or look for allegorical interpreta-tions: we never actually ''see'' the tiger; we don't ''hear'' Alina Reyes again once her transformation has occurred. Consequently, there is also less of a closure in those stories than there is in ''Axolotl,'' ''Night,'' or ''Idol.'' In the *End of the Game* stories there is no room left for our hesitation to develop or for other interpretations of the uncanny or supernatural occurrence than the one being unfolded by the narrative from the very beginning. Thus, they also fall outside allegorical literature.

Let me stress once again that the *End of the Game* stories are no less realistic in appearance than the *Bestiario* ones. The frame story in each case (the drunkard talking to the narrator of ''Flower,'' Somoza's fascina-tion with the idol, the obsession of ''Axolotl'' 's narrator with the strange animal, or the motorcyclist's reactions to his situation) is as solidly grounded in everyday reality as are the stories of the first book.

The last two stories of the first section of *End of the Game*, ''The Condemned Door'' and ''The Maenads,'' require some special attention. The latter tells, in a humorous tone, of how an over-enthusiastic crowd of music fans literally devours their beloved maestro. Obviously, this impossible ending is not intended to posit the intrusion of the supernatural, but to poke fun at a provincial society (the ''Corona'' theater of the story seems to represent the Teatro Colón of Buenos Aires) playing the role of the music lover.

"The Condemned Door" is a true fantastic story of the terror type, like Borges' "There Are More Things," where the affirmation of the supernatural causes fear. A salesman staying in a Montevideo hotel has been annoyed for two consecutive nights by the crying of a sick infant in the room next door. Blaming the noise on the woman living in that room who he thinks is a hysteric who imitates the weeping of a baby and then tries to calm the nonexistent baby down, the protagonist mimics the crying. The woman leaves the hotel the following morning. And that night, of course, Petrone hears the baby still crying in the empty room. The masterfully developed suspense of this story ends up, in its last paragraph, provoking the shock characteristic of ghost stories, as the protagonist, who has all along been adapting unconsciously to the presence of the supernatural, is forced to accept it fully, and flees the room in terror. The thoroughly realistic environment depicted in the story (the activities of the salesman, the middle-class hotel) makes the effect of its ending, no matter how well prepared we are for it, particularly strong.

Of the stories in the following book, *The Secret Weapons* (1959), only the title story can be called fantastic, and it is definitely of the passage type. In it, as in some of the stories discussed above, the supernatural communication that takes place does not cast doubt on the solidity of everyday reality, but is presented as a "natural" phenomenon. The passage between two states of being is developed in this story not in a dreamlike atmosphere ("Night") nor through an anguished search ("Axolotl," "Idol"), but slowly and in broad daylight, so to speak. Pierre, a Parisian student, gradually turns into the German soldier who seven years before had raped Michèle, who is now his girlfriend. We leave him as he, now fully possessed by the personality of the rapist, is ready to possess, all the time despising her, the woman whom he had loved and who was ready to offer herself to him. Meanwhile, a friend of Michèle's, Roland, whose wife the frightened girl had called for help as she became increasingly wary of her boyfriend's behavior, prepares to kill *again* the German he and other friends had executed after he raped Michèle the first time.[17] The transformation of the character into another—his real?—being, is achieved in this story as in "Night" independently of his wishes. And here too, the protagonist fights the change, but without the anguish that, together with the action-filled events (flight, capture, sacrifice) served in "Night" to underline as the absolute focus of the narrative the extraordinary transformation of the motorcyclist into the pre-Columbian warrior (or vice versa). In "Weapons," the narrator's attention concentrates instead on the psychological reactions of both protagonists to the changes taking place in one of them, Pierre. The consequence is a diminishing of the supernatural effect in favor of full acceptance of the transformation process. This effect is further diminished because our cooperation as readers is required constantly to discover what is happening, as in a mystery or detective story. In "Night," on the other hand, we are faced from the beginning with an impossible transformation that has already taken place and which the story's protagonist—and we as readers along with him—strive to shake off as a nightmare, to escape the supernatural's grip.

"Letters from Mamma" is a realistic story, a psychological portrait which, nevertheless, more closely approaches the classical fantastic than does "Weapons," though without ever entering it. A mother writes to her son and daughter-in-law, who have been living in Paris for two years, with news of her other son, who had died before the couple left Argentina. She then announces that Nico (the dead son) is traveling to France, and informs his brother and sister-in-law of the date of his arrival. At that moment the hesitation that is the fantastic's most characteristic feature appears and takes hold of the narrative. The protagonists, who had been trying to ignore *mamá*'s letters, go separately to the Saint-Lazare station in order to wait for the train from L'Havre. One of the disembarking passengers, seen from behind, resembles the dead Nico. But when the couple see his face they realize that they don't know the man. Why is it then that that night, as he gives up trying to write to his mother, Luis asks his wife: "Don't you think that he is much thinner?" To which she answers: "A little. One changes" (174).

The passage that the mere possibility of the supernatural had managed to open is kept open in "Letters," but with the full knowledge on the part of the protagonists of why this is done. Playing along with *mamá*'s fantasy will serve to appease Nico's brother's feelings of guilt for having stolen Laura, his wife, precisely at the time when Nico was dying of tuberculosis. (Laura too has not been able to forget what happened, to the point that she has nightmares about Nico.)

"The Other Heaven," a novella-length story that closes the next book, *All Fires the Fire* (1966), is, of all the stories by Cortázar having to do with passages in time and/or between worlds, the one that is most explicit about its subject. It not only thoroughly illustrates this theme in its plot, but actually reproduces it literally by having a good portion of the action take place in those covered shopping streets called *passages* or galleries.

A beautifully written story that blends with marvelous skill psychological description, autobiographical evocation,[18] and dramatic action, "The Other Heaven" is a passage story in which the opening of the door does not lead to death nor cause any kind of anguish. Instead it is viewed with a certain detachment, as something that although it no longer occurs for him, provides the protagonist-narrator with a refuge of happy memories. Notice that this story deals not only with the opening to the passage and what is revealed by a glance into the other side, but mainly, and at great length, with the world that lies at the other end of the passage, which in other stories is seen only in dramatic glimpses. And that world proves to be not different in nature—although it is, of course, considerably richer—from the quotidian one. But the most extraordinary thing about it is the ease with which it can be reached, at least at first; thus, the absolute absence of anxiety about finding it.

A thirty-year-old Buenos Aires stockbroker of the twentieth century is in the habit of entering, just by turning into this or that street, a section of Paris near the Bourse during the late eighteen-sixties. There he befriends a prostitute and makes many friends among the people of her circle, with whom he spends many fulfilling hours, very often in the *passages* of that area of the city. This nocturnal existence compensates for the protagonist's dull job and his bourgeois existence in general. Then the passage, which used to appear almost at will, becomes progressively more difficult to find, and longer and longer periods of time elapse between the protagonist's visits with Josiane and her friends, who include the poet Lautréamont.[19] Finally, he realizes, around the time when the Second World War is ending and the Franco-Prussian War is about to start in his other environment, that the galleries do not await him any longer. He begins only half willingly to spend more time with his mother and his fiancée, devotes more attention to his work, and after a brief but immensely happy return to his Paris existence, he forces himself not to think again of his "reconquered heaven" (196), and he marries Irma. (Cortázar uses similar language in "The Gates of Heaven," where Celina is described as being in "her hard won heaven" [*Bestiario* 138].)

Although he still hopes that the passage is not closed to him forever, the narrator thinks that the deaths of "the South-American" (Lautréamont) and the serial killer who used to be the terror of Josiane and her friends are related to what he terms his own death. A "death" whose peacefulness, however, suggests that the notion of a passage between two states of consciousness is no longer felt by Cortázar with the almost neurotic urgency that had informed his previous representations of that passage. This does not mean, of course, that the author of "The Other Heaven" thinks, like the character he creates in that story, that the passage is closed to him. Not being a bourgeois in the same sense as the story's protagonist, he is freer and better equipped to continue pursuing the opening into the mysterious passage. And yet one cannot help but think that Cortázar might have felt that somehow this door was becoming elusive for him too, and that, as with the reluctant stockbroker, a cycle in his life and in his art was ending. This would account for the vividness with which "The Other Heaven" illustrates its subject (the passage) and the force and richness of its portrayal of the world reached by that passage.[20] The artist who had so persistently devoted his energy to crossing to "the other side" seems to be saying farewell to that "heaven" in this novella, whose importance for his work is as great as that of "The Pursuer."[21]

After having expressed his belief in an opening into another world in such powerful, dramatic ways that his whole work became identified with that passage—as confirmed by critical statements which we will examine shortly—Cortázar moved in the direction of simply pointing to the existence of the passage as an almost normal phenomenon. Notwithstanding what he himself has said about finding the passage more or less casually, just by being always ready to encounter the door into it, the search for or the transit through the passage was accompanied in "Idol," "Axolotl," "Night," and "Weapons" by tremendous anxiety. This anxiety seems to have disappeared by the time "The Other Heaven" was written. And thus the irrational, identified as the only force capable of opening the gate to the passage, and the distinguishing mark of so much of Cortázar's work, including his best novel, *Hopscotch* (1963), is replaced by the imagination, a power, and more commonly a faculty or capacity that can be regulated at least to some extent. Witness the way "The Other Heaven"'s protagonist knows the general location of his private opening to the world of dream and applies to his search for it a method of his own device. Naturally, the trained artist will carry on that search more effectively and also more consciously.

Changes in Cortázar's life that facilitated an easier adjustment to the world may have contributed to the diminishing presence of anguish as a response to that passage in his work.[22] Parallel to those developments, a growing awareness on Cortázar's part of the social fabric and of history would develop into a political commitment, the first signs of which are already present in *All Fires*.[23] That commitment would contribute eventually to a reduction in the importance within his work of the role of the passage, which by definition escapes reason, and consequently, also history. Finally—since once the search for the passage stops being so anguished, it allows reason to help in its pursuit—it also becomes open to the influence of history; or rather, it tries to appropriate history for its own goal. This is what happens in the novel *A Manual for Manuel* (1973). The result is a more explicit control by the artist of his search for an opening to "the other side."

Of the stories that precede "The Other Heaven" in *All Fires the Fire*, only "The Island at Noon" deals with a supernatural passage between two realms. The "fantastic accepted"—since a supernatural type of communication is accomplished here—consists in "The Island" of a vision experienced by an airplane steward who has been dreaming for a long time of a visit to a Greek island that he sees regularly from the plane. Marini sees himself arriving on the island, deciding to stay there forever, watching his plane fall into the sea, and finally rescuing a dying man who is actually himself, since he was on board the aircraft when the accident took place.

In her book on magical realism, Chanady points out that the abrupt change in the last lines of the narrative "from the free indirect discourse that conveyed Marini's thoughts to the commentary of [a] ... spectator" (63) underlines the presence of the supernatural by suggesting that as the injured steward dies, his "spirit can no longer observe what [is] going on around him" (6), as it was doing before, with the attention to realistic detail characteristic of the vision of someone who is very much alive. The introduction of an outside perspective to replace that of the now dead steward confirms the occurrence of the supernatural. Instead of the passage serving to facilitate a real transformation, it simply serves in "The Island" to make real, however briefly, the protagonist's most fervent desire, which includes a rejection of modern civilization and a return to nature. Marini's visit to the island resembles the visits to the world of the *passages* undertaken again and again by the protagonist of "The Other Heaven," also made possible through the power of a very active imagination.

Although it has the appearance of being a passage story, the title story, "All Fires the Fire," falls completely outside the fantastic since there is not even the suggestion in it of a connection between the two stories told simultaneously by the narrator, one superimposed on the other. In one, with a contemporary Parisian setting, a man involved with two women starts a fire as a result of his negligence, which most likely will cause his death and that of the woman with whom he is in bed at the moment. In the other story, a proconsul's wife desires a handsome gladiator. The proconsul, aware of his wife's desire, arranges for the gladiator to fight an almost invincible opponent so that he will be killed; this will most likely be the fate of the proconsul and his wife, too, victims of a fire (perhaps caused by sparks from a nearby volcano, maybe Vesuvius, as in *The Last Days of Pompeii*?) that is spreading to the entire circus.

"The Southern Thruway" is a fantastic story of a different kind than the "passage" ones. One Sunday afternoon the incoming traffic on the *autoroute du Sud* comes to a complete halt between Fontainebleau and Paris. First hours, and then days, weeks, and months go by without the cars being able to advance more than a few meters. This forces their occupants, whom the narrator calls by the names of their cars, not only to establish contact with each other, but to organize themselves in groups in order to obtain water and food and to help the sick. As whatever caused the traffic jam goes away and the cars start to move forward, to increase speed, to separate, the protagonist mourns the rapid disappearance of the group that had been created, and more particularly that of the woman whom he had been making love to and who now carries their child. He wishes that the community that had been formed, and that seemed more real than the lives they all lived before, could be reconstructed. But instead, there is now a mad rushing "among unknown cars in which noone knew anything about the others and where everyone looked fixedly and exclusively forward" (*All Fires* 42).

The protagonist's regret at the superficiality of personal contacts imposed by modern civilization—for which the busy superhighway is an ideal image—defines the use of the fantastic in this story as allegorical. The development of the allegory is carried out here, however, in an unusual way, since it only becomes apparent, and this rather explicitly, at the end, in the final sentences of the text, taking us a little by surprise. The narrative's concentration on the relationships fostered by that peculiar traffic jam, and the pace of the action, which is structurally tied to the movement of the vehicles stuck on the highway, is not hampered in any way by the almost secret development of the allegorical meaning of the story.

"La autopista" pretends to be a strictly realistic story about the consequences of an extraordinary highway accident. The fantastic element creeps into the action through the impossible prolongation and the unknown cause of the superhighway's paralysis, thus provoking in the reader the fantastic's characteristic hesitation regarding the plausibility of the supernatural event. This situation persists until the hours have stretched into months, while all along, the drivers accept their immobility in spite of the lack of food, water, or appropriate shelter. The reader, however, does not begin to look immediately—as he does in "Letter to a Young Lady in Paris" when faced with an equally impossible event—for alternative, non-fantastic, and most likely allegorical readings of the story. This is due to the close involvement of the narrative with the human situation it paints, an involvement which develops realistically and with many dramatic turns independently of the supernatural basis of that situation.

"La autopista" 's message concerning commitment to other people's needs
as the only way to avoid the extinction of mankind points to Cortázar's
move in the direction of a definite political involvement.

This move is further stressed in another allegorical story, "Instructions for John Howell," also of *All Fires*. "Instructions" belongs within
the unexplained uncanny rather than the fantastic. In it a man is practically
forced, under more or less veiled threats, to perform as an actor in the
second act of a play that he has been attending in a London theater. He
receives a secret request from his leading lady: "Don't let them kill me"
(134), and later on: "Stay with me until the end" (140). During the third
act (for the second, the protagonist was told simply to improvise his inter-
ventions), he goes against the careful instructions that he is given for his
performance as Howell, and as a result is violently thrown out of the play
at the end of the act. He then watches as, in the fourth and final act, the
actor who had played the role of Howell before he was forced to do so
stops Eva, his wife in the play, from drinking a poisoned cup of tea; but
the latter dies anyway. Upon witnessing this, the protagonist flees the
theater, while "Howell" also leaves the stage running. The two men meet
in the typically deserted streets and alleys of the London of mystery stories
and movies. To the protagonist's self-questioning about Eva's dramatic
plea, his own behavior during the third act, directed at preventing her
death, and his unjustified fear, "Howell" has no answer but to say: "It
is always the same. . . . This is typical of the amateurs, they think they
can do better than the others [to save Eva, as Rice, the protagonist, had
tried to do], and at the end it is useless" (146); i.e., the ones in control
succeed in their plan to kill her. And since the sound of the whistles of
their pursuers is getting closer, the two fugitives start to run again, going,
at Howell's urging, in different directions, since there is more of a chance
that way that at least one of them will manage to escape. These uncanny
events—which are, nevertheless not supernatural (the presumed death of
Eva as the result of maneuvers by those who try to keep her from communicating with her stage husband could very well be part of the play)—point
clearly to the need for all men of good will to become involved, even if
it appears fruitless, in the fight against the evil conspiracies that otherwise
would make use of them. By acting irresponsibly, simply following the
whims of his ego, the protagonist of the story has brought upon himself
a curse that will pursue him forever. When observed more closely, however, the signs received by the protagonist, Rice, prove to be contradictory:
he is first told to improvise (for the second act), and then given detailed
instructions (for the third). But although he does his best at improvising

during the second act, Rice's actions and answers respond in fact to questions and comments that come from a text that the actors have memorized. Then, in the next act, he not only resists following the instructions alluded to in the story's title, but actually works against them. The only thing that remains constant regarding the development of the two acts in which Rice is a performer, is Eva's plea for help. But because of his refusal to follow the instructions that he has been given, Rice cannot do what the woman secretly asks him to do during the third act: "Stay with me until the end"; and she is killed.

Such contradictions are indicative of Cortázar's own struggle, especially acute at the time the *All Fires* stories were written, with his social *pris de concience*,[24] his conflict between the desire to maintain his individuality as a writer in its purest form—i.e., his right to experiment and play, independent of any political commitment—and the need to comply with political directives which might be restrictive and even incomprehensible as far as their purpose, but which are supposed to have been devised for the common good. The demand to adapt one's work to one's *engagement* is represented in *A Manual for Manuel* (1973) through the dream in which the novel's protagonist agrees to carry out a mission the nature of which he cannot remember. He tells his wife of a dream he has just had in which, while watching Fritz Lang's movie, "M," he is summoned to leave the movie hall—something that annoys him, since he wants very much to see that "mystery" film—in order to meet a Cuban. The next scene of the dream is the result of the interview, the mission that Andrés has been charged with but does not understand (*Libro de Manuel* 101–3).

Is a happy compromise between the need for creative play and the commitment to work for the transformation of society possible before the victim (Eva, the captive Third World, the oppressed of the earth) is sacrificed? Rice's mad flight suggests that there is no solution to that dilemma. But his wish to know ("I cannot go on fleeing forever, without knowing" [147]) points toward a solution to his predicament. The story that we read, no matter how little conscious of this fact the writer might be, constitutes an answer to this dilemma insofar as Cortázar identifies the antagonists in that struggle through writing about it, and thus facilitates reaching an understanding of the problem he faces and finding meaningful solutions to it in his own art. One of these could be to pursue precisely the ambiguity exemplified by the contradictory signals received by Rice.

Cortázar's next collection of short stories, *Octahedron* (1974), includes one, "Severo's Phases," situated between the uncanny and the supernatural. This "rite," as it is classified in *Los relatos*, describes a very strange ritual:

the narrator gathers one evening with other men and women (and even a child) at a friend's house in order to witness him undergo a series of "phases" (sweating, jumping, assigning numbers to people, telling them to advance or slow their watches, attracting moths to his face, and, finally, sleeping with a handkerchief over his face) which are described as things that everyone has to experience at some time. Although in fact nothing happens in the story that could be called supernatural, the series of acts being watched by the narrator and the others is so utterly extraordinary and without explanation that we tend to link them to the supernatural, perhaps as a kind of *passage* into it. "Phases" resembles "Cefalea," a "game" according to *Los relatos*' classification. Like the task of caring for the mancuspias, the central event of "Phases," although it is described as a commonplace occurrence, remains undecipherable. The connections it has to reality (a wake, the agony of a dying man) are denied both by Severo's actions themselves and by the witnesses' reactions to them.

What could be the explanation of those "phases" that Severo has to experience and that the narrator seems to fear he will soon have to undergo? As in "Cefalea," the text remains utterly mute regarding the meaning of its subject. Our guesses as to what the phases might signify are not validated in any way by the words of the story itself; yet we feel certain that, since the supernatural, which may be an end in itself, does not play a role in this story, the strange events described in it must lead to an allegorical meaning. That meaning, however, is at least as elusive as in some of Kafka's narratives, if not even more so.

Two other *Octahedron* stories suggest the fantastic, but do not in fact fall within the genre. In "Summer," a wild horse seems to want to enter the summer house of a couple whose relationship has deteriorated into a dull routine, but who end up making love as the husband forces his frightened wife back to bed. This makes him reflect that the horse, representing a renewal of their love, may actually have entered the house through the door left open by the little girl that they are taking care of that day (an "innocent" capable of opening a passage into the extraordinary).

"Throat of a Black Kitten" is reminiscent of the non-fantastic *Bestiario* story "Circe," whose protagonist shares with the protagonist of "Throat" a schizophrenic reaction to male suitors. It also bears a resemblance to "Do Not Blame Anyone," since it includes the suggestion that the body's movements can be initiated totally independently of the subject's will. The way the hands of Dina, the protagonist, seem to acquire a life and will of their own in order to touch other people in cafes and metro cars, and the way those hands become at the end like the claws of a cat in order to scratch the male protagonist in the dark—while the unseen presence of the girl is felt for a second to be that of a feline—suggest the supernatural. But it is Dina's, and not a cat's neck that her companion grabs. In the final account the story is about the loneliness and isolation characteristic of life in a modern metropolis (Paris), which is what drives Dina to establish those brief contacts that only lead to shame and humiliation and prevent her from engaging in a relationship of the type that the male protagonist, yet another one of Cortázar's Latin Americans in Paris, offers her.

Only one of the stories that make up *Someone Walking Around* (*Alguien que anda por ahí*, 1977) belongs to the fantastic. "Encounter Within a Red Circle" is a terror-type story strongly reminiscent of Borges' terror story "There Are More Things"—and also, of course, of Cortázar's own "The Condemned Door." But the terror provoked in the latter story comes as more of a surprise, and, because of that and the fact that the suspense in it is developed within a thoroughly realistic setting, is more effective too. The supernatural is not limited in "Encounter" to a single frightening presence that becomes evident at the end of the narrative, but includes ceremonies, tortures, vampires, the living dead. Even if all of this is only suggested at the conclusion of the story, it makes of "Encounter" a much more traditional and even mass audience-oriented fantastic story than any other by its author.

Even in this simple text, however, Cortázar displays his characteristically novelistic propensity for developing the psychological dynamics between the characters. The story is told in the form of an oral letter addressed to the protagonist by the nearsighted English woman he feels he has somehow to protect from the threatening looks of the hostess and waiters of the sinister-looking Balkan restaurant where they are the only customers. The protagonist follows the woman when she leaves the restaurant and then, inexplicably, goes back to it. There the hostess and the waiters are awaiting his return in order to resume the ceremony in which the woman had previously been the victim. She is a weak living-dead who tried to prevent the protagonist from falling into the same trap into which she once fell. Now that there are two of them, they might be more successful in saving others, she thinks.

Of course, one could interpret this story as one more instance of the search for a passage into the unknown; but the fact remains that in "Encounter" the hesitation and the supernatural are too much of the "Fright Night" variety. This drastically reduces the impact of any serious concern that the story might have other than simply provoking fear.

(Vampirism was the subject of considerable attention by Cortázar in

62. A Model Kit [1968], a novel whose narrative structure follows the model for a novel proposed in the sixty-second chapter of *Hopscotch*. Images of and references to vampirism begin to appear from the beginning of the narrative. The protagonist, Juan, imagines—or perhaps just plays with the possibility—that a mysterious-looking old woman who is a guest at the same Viennese hotel where he and his girlfriend are staying is a historical Hungarian countess who was accused of vampirism in the eighteenth century, and whom the novel has by that time mentioned several times. Convinced that the vampire intends to seduce another guest at the hotel, an English girl whose naiveté makes her strongly reminiscent of the English woman of "Encounter," Juan follows the two women into the girl's room, and actually witnesses the old lady undressing the apparently hypnotized girl. By that time, though, the scene is taking on a definitely oneiric quality: Juan and his lover are in the room with the vampire and her potential victim, talking freely about what they are seeing without being heard or seen. This oneiric quality is further stressed in the epilogue to the sequence, in which the protagonist follows Frau Marta and the girl into a city square full of trams, and eventually steps off the one on which they are all traveling by now into a Buenos Aires street, just before returning to the room where his friend is waiting for him. The only seemingly supernatural—since our hesitation is resolved here in favor of the reality of the vampire—element of this section of *62* is further weakened within the larger context of the novel by its connection with the attempted seduction of the young Celia by Hélène, the woman the protagonist loves, which is taking place at the same time in Paris. Vampirism seems to stand in *62* as a paradigm of misguided love relationships.)

Several stories of the next book, *We Love Glenda So Much* (1980), strongly suggest the fantastic, although in fact only two fall within Todorov's definition of the genre. "Text in a Notebook" is a first-person account of a mysterious conspiracy by a group of people (a sect?), aimed at taking over the Buenos Aires subway system. The "text"'s author, who has discovered the plot and is killed at the end by the conspirators, describes in fascinating detail the customs of the group, how they manage their existence underground, and how he thinks they are proceeding in their plan. The absurdity of the plan (what could be its purpose?) underscores the possibility that the entire account is but the hallucination of a neurotic (someone in fact like the author of the "Report on the Blind" in Ernesto Sábato's *On Heroes and Tombs*, a fantastic narrative describing the conspiracy of the blind to take over the entire world). While in "Letter to a Young Lady in Paris,'' for example, the virtual impossibility of the central event acts to shorten the duration of the hesitation in the direction of dismissing the existence of the bunnies even before one discovers the traces of madness in the narrator's account, the nature of the underground conspiracy of ''Text in a Notebook'' falls within a category of the impossible closer to some form of acceptability.

At the end of ''Orientation of Cats,'' the story that opens *We Like Glenda So Much*, there is a brief suggestion of a fantastic passage, when the narrator feels as if Alana, who has been absorbed in the contemplation of a certain picture, is not really ''back'' when she turns her face toward him, but has in fact gone inside the picture in order to look forever at whatever the cat depicted in the picture is watching.

In ''Story with *Migalas*'' (a type of spider), a male voice is heard in a hotel room in which at first only two women seem to be living, and which is supposedly empty after their departure. The two women who are the protagonists of the story and who are staying in the next room connect that voice with another male at a faraway farm where they had met in order to plan a crime, and where the killing of that same man apparently took place. It is thus hinted that the man next door may be the dead Michael, haunting those who thought until now that they were at a safe distance from their crime. But in fact the voice could also belong to a real person; and the protagonists (whom we leave as they prepare—by, first of all, undressing—to meet that presence that follows them) could very well be hallucinating. The story calls to mind ''Story with a Water Background,'' which also suggests the supernatural without actually making us confront it.

The suggestion of the supernatural in ''Story with *Migalas*'' implies, of course, a passage between the worlds of the dead and the living. ''Stories That I Tell Myself'' also deals with a passage, albeit one of a limited and down-to-earth nature. A man who has self-induced erotic dreams in which he fantasizes himself as a truck driver has a dream involving a woman who, along with her husband, is a close friend of the protagonist and his wife. In the dream he picks her up on a road by her disabled car, and then, almost at her request, makes love to her. And this is exactly what happens to Dilia soon afterwards, but with a ''real'' truck driver. Consequently, she does not acknowledge the protagonist-narrator's desire for her when he tells her that he knows the second part of the story (she has told her friends about the accident and her being saved by a truck driver), but confesses to him that she slept with her rescuer. Since both the narrator's erotic dream and its object's brief affair are perfectly possible, their coincidence does not have to be seen as fantastic.

The passage theme is presented in a much more sophisticated form in "Press Clippings." An Argentinean writer living in Paris, this one a woman (an unusual choice for Cortázar, all of whose Latin Americans-in-Paris before this had been men; a choice suggestive of a deliberate search for a woman's perspective and thus, of an opening to women's concerns in a writer who has been accused of exhibiting patriarchal attitudes),[25] goes to see a sculptor, also Argentinean, who has asked her to write a text to introduce a series of sculptures on the theme of violence. The writer gives the sculptor a newspaper account of the kidnapping, torture, and assassination by the Army, for political reasons, of several members of a Buenos Aires family. Both friends complain of being impotent to do anything about such crimes. Their occupying themselves with art and writing appears very frivolous as a result. Upon leaving the studio, the protagonist-narrator meets a little girl, who, crying, takes her to the room where her father is slowly torturing her mother by burning her with a cigarette. The protagonist knocks the man down with a chair, unties the wife and, remembering the brutal facts described in the Latin American newspaper, helps the woman to tie her husband so that she, and perhaps also the protagonist herself, can torture him.

An account of what follows, of being momentarily "on the other side of the cut-off hands and the common graves" (*Queremos* 78) is what the writer gives her friend as the text to accompany the catalogue of his sculptures. Then, she finds out two or three days later from a newspaper clipping that the sculptor sends her, that what she witnessed had actually taken place—or was taking place at the same time that she experienced it—in Marseille instead of in Paris. The narrator rushes to the scene of her experience, but cannot find the house, which was pictured in the newspaper article. However, the little girl, whose disappearance was mentioned in the account of the crime, is exactly where she first met her; and her surname corresponds to that of the dead man in the newspaper account.

By means of a supernatural passage through space and possibly also through time (if the child's spirit preceded her body to Paris: the concierge who is keeping the girl until a social worker comes for her does not clarify when it was that she found her, although the implication is that this occurred earlier the same day), the protagonist becomes fully conscious, with an overwhelming feeling of immediacy, of the physical and spiritual effects of torture. The torture which she first witnesses and then participates in belongs to the same type of violence that so many of her compatriots were—and continue to be, if we extend the term to all Latin Americans—the victims of. That the actions in which Noemí, the protagonist, participates are of a purely private instead of a political nature matters little in terms of their overall significance in relation to man's role as his fellow man's wolf in all political and geographical latitudes—which is the subject of the works that the sculptor asked his friend to introduce. The little girl's innocence, which would make it impossible for her to distinguish between the realms of the public and the private, bridges the gap separating them; it also facilitates, as in "Bestiary," the passage from reality to the supernatural. Meanwhile the protagonist becomes an avenger, in the context of a domestic tragedy (which is representative of the oppression of women by men) of all victims of political violence. But she becomes a torturer as well.

"Clippings" is not only highly original in terms of its use of the fantastic passage in order to underscore the horrors of political torture (it does this by enacting them in a context where they can reach the protagonist as well as most people), but also in terms of its structure as a fantastic story. What seems at first a realistic event is suddenly revealed to be of a supernatural nature. The doubt as to whether in fact Noemí experienced what she tells her friend and the reader (we are also the addressees of the text she writes recounting her experience) is introduced at the same time as the supernatural character of the incident. This is done by the sculptor, who sends the protagonist the newspaper clipping about the Marseille "drama," along with his congratulations for her dramatic abilities, i.e., for feigning that what he assumes she copied from the papers was a real experience. Meeting the little girl firmly establishes Noemí's account, now completed as the story that we have been reading all along, on the side of the supernatural.

This superb fantastic story turns out also to be very effective as a statement about political commitment, an indication that Cortázar was reaching, by the time he wrote "Clippings," the full use of his political voice. This is confirmed by "Nightmares," one of the stories in the next collection, *Deshoras* (1982), which takes place against the background of the "dirty war" in Argentina.

In *Deshoras* (*Suddenly*), Cortázar's last book of short stories (1982), there is only one text in which the supernatural plays a role. "End of a Period" (*Fin de etapa*) tells of the visit by a lonely woman who has recently broken up with her lover or husband to an art exhibit in the museum of a small town. All of the paintings, distributed among three rooms, reproduce the same table and chair, shown in several rooms of the same house. In the last painting, which occupies the third room all by itself, there is a woman sitting at the table; her peculiar immobility suggests that she is dead, her death being indeed the natural culmination of the silence and loneliness which are the theme of the other paintings. Before seeing the last picture, which she has left to do during her last visit to the museum after lunch, the protagonist, while wandering through the town, visits the house pictured in all the paintings. In the third room of the house there is a table with an empty chair next to it. We leave the protagonist sitting at that table, motionless, and waiting, almost certainly, for a passage to her own death. The passivity of the character, who accepts all those coincidences as fitting her depressed state of mind, prevents the appearance of any kind of hesitation regarding them. Fear too plays a minimal role in the story, arising only when Diane, after hearing someone laugh, flees the enchanted house to which she will return later in order to die, if only metaphorically, in the sense of a spiritual death.

Some may argue that many other stories in the collections reviewed above are also fantastic, e.g., "After Lunch," "The Band," and even "End of the Game," in the book by that title; "The Pursuer," "Blow-Up," "The Good Services," in *The Secret Weapons*; "The Health of the Sick," "Nurse Cora," and "Meetings," of *All Fires the Fire*; "A Place Named Kindberg," "Liliana Weeping," "There But Where, How," and "Manuscript Found in a Pocket," in *Octahedron*; "A Change of Light," "Trade Winds," "You Laid Down at His Side," "In the Name of Bobby," "Apocalypse at Solentiname," "The Ferry, or Another Trip to Venice," "The Faces of the Medal," in *Someone Walking Around*; "Grafitti," "Clone," "Moebius Strip," of *We Love Glenda So Much*; "The School at Night," "Nightmares," "Satarsa," in *Deshoras*. And indeed some of those texts suggest the fantastic through the relative improbability of the events narrated in them as well as by means of their oneiric tone, while others undoubtedly deal with a communication between different states of consciousness. However, in none of those stories, some of which are definitely allegorical (with political intentions in "Grafitti" and "Nightmares," both particularly effective as political narratives) is the supernatural ever suggested even in passing. The passage in them is something alluded to rather than a reality.

I noted above that the 1970 edition of Cortázar's short stories, *Los relatos*, divides them into "rites," "games," and "passages," and includes some texts that were not part of the collections published before. Some of those stories are fantastic or at least point to the fantastic rather forcefully. "With Authentic Pride," a "rite," is a story after the manner of Kafka, to whom it is dedicated. Its meaning, beyond the obvious allusion to the effects of the bureaucratic state on our minds, seems, as in Kafka's stories, to become more and more elusive as the reader tries to unveil it. A first-person narrator tells of the law that, in the city where he lives, has since ancient times regulated the gathering of the dead leaves. All the citizens, including the children and the elderly, have to participate in this rather complicated job involving the use of mongooses and a snake's smell. Otherwise—although in fact noone ever thinks of not ful- filling his duty regarding such a beneficial law—they would be sent to the jungles in order to look for snakes.

"The Trip" is not strictly a fantastic story, but its ominous, and also Kafka-like, atmosphere suggests that the supernatural may make an appearance at any moment through the protagonist's total inability to remember where it is that he is supposed to travel that day.

"The Season of the Hand"—a "game"—is a very early story, resur- rected by the author from the period prior to the composition of *Bestiario*.[26] Its use of the fantastic (a hand comes to visit the narrator every afternoon, becoming his best friend for a while) is of the allegorical kind: the protagonist eventually becomes afraid of the hand, which repre- sents the imagination, thinking that it may cut off his own left hand in order to be with it (it is a right hand). On realizing that she is feared, the hand leaves, never to come back, and the protagonist, who is also the narrator, returns to his prior bourgeois existence.

"Silvia," although officially a "rite," is a typical passage story that includes Cortázar's characteristic interest in the behavior and the minds of children. The narrator, who appears to be Cortázar himself, is able twice to see and almost make love to Silvia, an imaginary adolescent girl invented by the children of his friends as their companion.

"The Deepest Caress" is another Kafka-like story about a man who one day, all of a sudden, discovers that he has begun to sink into the earth. The process of sinking continues for several weeks without anyone noticing it, until the protagonist finally disappears into the earth.

We should consider, finally, and very briefly, whether the delightful vignettes that make up the book called *Historias de cronopios y famas* (1962) could be considered to belong to the fantastic. Some of the outra- geous acts described in those very funny short tales and scenes are fantas- tic in nature. But it would be wrong to include within the category of the fantastic texts which are not meant to cast doubt on reality, but rather, to reveal what lies beyond the "sticky" mass of everyday behaviors, pursu- ing the humorous possibilities in them, or to "instruct" us in doing the unexpected. *Cronopios*, *famas*, and *esperanzas* stand, obviously, for various types of people and of human reactions, with the *cronopios* representing Cortázar's ideal of total freedom from bourgeois constraints and prejudices, as well as from responsibilities.

Like Borges, Cortázar has contributed some theoretical reflections to the definition of the fantastic. These are scattered in essays, interviews, and the impressionistic texts that make up the books *Around the Day in Eighty Worlds* (1967) and *Last Round* (1969). Those comments are much more the spontaneous expression of the writer's concerns as his wandering mind considers different aspects of writing than, as in Borges' case, a deliberate attempt to explain the fantastic.

Two main ideas run through those statements, serving to unify them. One is the identification of the fantastic with an access to the unknown, to attain which, it is necessary to let down all our defenses and allow the unconscious to dominate our thinking and, by extension, our writing as well. The other recurring notion posits erasing all distinctions between the fantastic and the non-fantastic in Cortázar's writings. He would like to see his work as just one text which is always open to the possibility that the passage will appear.

Talking about early memories of his reaction to literature, Cortázar remarks that he was surprised at a schoolmate's calling "fantastic" a story about an invisible man, which he himself had interpreted, because of an almost innate disposition to "suspend disbelief," as thoroughly possible.[27] That approach results in his seeking in his own fiction a kind of osmosis between the fantastic and the quotidian, so that one could move naturally from the latter into the former (*Ultimo round* 1:82).

At the same time, Cortázar notes that it was through "an act of will, a choice" on his part (*Ultimo round* 1:70) that he absorbed the fantastic from life. That intense "familiarity with the fantastic" (71) is what permits the artist who has become, because of it, open to a reality that others do not see, to transform the world radically. Because the fantastic is everywhere, Cortázar does not think anymore, as he once did, that it functions in a fatal way, according to rules apart from normal physical causality. The writer is clearly referring to the supernatural, which is not, he insists, "closed" (73) or predetermined in its development, as in many fantastic stories, but belongs to a much larger order, permanently ready to disrupt ordinary reality.

Some observations by Cortázar on the technique of the fantastic story agree with Todorov's analysis of the genre. The good fantastic story requires "an ordinary temporal development" (*Ultimo round* 1:79) into which the fantastic (the supernatural) irrupts only for an instant, but in such a way that "the exceptional becomes the rule without displacing the ordinary structures within which it has inserted itself" (80). In other words, ordinary reality has to be fully permeated by the spirit of the fantastic, yet without losing its nature as happens in the worst type of fantastic literature through a kind of total takeover of the narrative by the supernatural (81).

To the prohibition implied by the supernatural against entering its realm, Cortázar answers with a move precisely to open that door. This should not be difficult to accomplish, since the gate, lying as it does under our own eyelids, is readily accessible through dreams. Let us fall asleep into the heart of the first dream, proposes Cortázar, and we will be able to enter a second dream and awake inside it (*Ultimo round* 1:170–72). The writer's method for opening the door that leads to the "passage" is what he calls *distracción* (absentmindedness), which represents in his view a deeper form of attention and an opening to that which is normally ignored (*Ultimo round* 2:127–29, at 127).

In another text, Cortázar clarifies further his receptiveness to the passage by explaining how he is constantly "threatened" by "laterality" or a "parallax" (the displacement of an object because of the observer's position) vision, by being always more to the left or to the back of the place where one should be in order to lead a quiet, conflict-free life ("Del sentimiento" 35). The state of mind that the writer aims for is conceived in terms of a dream: "Very often I have felt that that tear within the wakeful state is a sort of passage through which reality shows the dimensions of a dream, that other way of being which is [still] in us when we wake up" (Bjurstrom 18). This, Cortázar continues, we have to translate when we remember it in terms of time and space, which are our only ways of understanding the world.

Because Cortázar sees his whole literary output as the expression of the search for another dimension of reality, he does not distinguish between his fantastic and non-fantastic texts: "Almost all the stories that I have written belong to the genre called, for lack of a better name, fantastic. They oppose that false realism consisting of believing that everything can be described and explained in the manner assumed by the scientific and philosophical optimism of the eighteenth century" ("Algunos aspectos" 262).

But if the passage leads the writer's consciousness to a dreamlike state capable of revealing a richer reality, that opening allows him at the same time to perform a kind of exorcism of the "invading creatures," which transforms them into a condition that while "giving them a universal existence, places them also at the other end of the bridge, where the narrator is no longer" (*Ultimo round* 1:66). Although these comments are contemporary with, or were at least published around the same time as some of the others, they point to the attitude that I discussed in relation to "The Other Heaven" as being indicative of a growing detachment regarding the passage, a distancing from it which does not imply, however, doubting its reality, as confirmed by the writer's last testimony on the passage's existence in "Paper Clippings."

Cortázar adds in the same statement that it is not an exaggeration to say that all successful short stories, and in particular fantastic stories (a category within which he would include all of his) "are neurotic products, nightmares or hallucinations that have been neutralized through their objectification and translation to an environment outside the neurotic one . . . as if the author had wanted to get rid radically and as soon as possible of his creature, exorcising it the only way that was available to him, by writing it out" (ibid.). These reflections come rather close to Todorov's identification of the fantastic—which for Cortázar is not limited to the supernatural—with the repressed, and of the genre in general with the bad conscience of a puritanic age.

Notes

1. After having said "uno de nosotros" (one of us, in the masculine)
   several times, the story's narrator says suddenly, "*una* de nosotros,"
   then goes back to "uno," but says once more "una," and then again
   "uno" (*Bestiario* 79, 84, 85, 87, 89).
2. Ibid., 90. The "cefalea" is a very strong headache, often recurrent and
   affecting only one side of the head, like a migraine. The story features
   a dedication to a physician whose "poem" on the cure of the cefalea
   provided "the most beautiful images" of the story. The author also
   thanks someone for having introduced him to the "mancuspias" (69).
3. It appeared in *Anales de Buenos Aires* 1.11 (1946). It is normally
   referred to as Cortázar's first published short story. See Sara de Mundo
   Lo, *Julio Cortázar*.
4. For instance, in José H. Brandt Rojas' "Asedios a 'Casa tomada'"
   General Perón, the leader of an extremely popular movement calling for
   social and economic reforms benefitting the workers, was elected president in 1946.
5. In the story "La banda," of *Final del juego* (1956), a man goes to a
   Buenos Aires movie theater in 1947 in order to see a certain famous
   film, but before this is shown he has to endure two awful, ridiculous
   performances by a band made up of female employees of a factory.
   Reflecting on what he has witnessed, he concludes that what had seemed
   incoherent and false was actually *the* reality. His whole life then appears
   foreign to him. A few months later he leaves Argentina for good. See
   Marta Morello-Frosch, " 'La banda' de los otros."
6. Antonio Planells, in " 'Casa tomada,' " sees the brother and sister as
   an incestuous couple expelled from Paradise for refusing to have any off-
   spring.
7. Noé Jitrik, in "Notas sobre la 'zona sagrada,' " sees in the *Bestiario*
   stories a movement to expel a "sacred zone" living inside the subject.
   Cortázar referred to the stories of his first book as "glimpses, dimensions, or hints of possibilities that terrified or fascinated me and that I
   had to exhaust by working them off in the story" (cited, from an interview with Luis Harss, in Evelyn Picón Garfield's *Julio Cortázar* 17).
   He says that "Casa tomada" sprang directly from a nightmare he had
   about being alone in a house, hearing a noise at the end of a corridor,
   closing a door and then hearing the noise on his side of the door (19).
   "Cefalea" is a transformation into artistic material of the migraine head-
   aches suffered by the writer (20), while "Carta a una señorita en París"
   reproduces the recurring nausea that he felt while studying to become

a public translator (23), and "Circe," his fear of finding bugs in his food (24).

8. Alazraki, noting that this is a story centered on a character rather than on a situation, as are most of the *Bestiario* stories, applies to "Distances" a Lacanian interpretation: Alina sees her acts as those of a false I (*En busca* 184–200).

9. Reminiscing about the story many years later, Cortázar refers to Luis and "el Nene" as brothers ("Noticias de los Funes," in *Ultimo round* 1:122).

10. Alazraki detects an erotic attraction for Rema on the part of Isabel, so that the tiger points not only to Nene's desire, but also to the girl's (*En busca* 175, 178).

11. "La caricia más profunda," "Estación de la mano," and "Con legítimo orgullo" were published in *La vuelta*, vol. 2; "Silvia" in *Ultimo round*, vol. 1, and "El viaje," ibid., vol. 2.

12. Antonio Risco sees this story as an example of the "pure fantastic" ("Lo fantástico en un cuento de Julio Cortázar").

13. Julio Ortega sees the story as dominated by the contamination of reality by the dream ("La dinámica de lo fantástico").

14. Of the "moteca" tribe (*Ceremonias* 135). The word, since no such people existed in ancient Mexico, suggests the motorcycle that the young man was riding. However, Cortázar makes fun of Roger Caillois' guess that the "motecas" were so named because the story's protagonist rode a motorcyle ("Una de tantas tardes de Saignon," *Ultimo round* 1:16–41, at 21). The story was inspired by an accident Cortázar had in 1952 while riding a Vespa (Evelyn Picón Garfield, *Julio Cortázar* 31).

15. He feels that the accident was like a hole, an empty space lasting an eternity, or rather "as if within that hole he had gone through something or traveled enormous distances" (136). Julio Ortega notes that the story employs three of the devices prescribed by Borges for fantastic literature: the double, travel in time, and contamination of reality by the dream ("La dinámica" 132).

16. See *Beyond the Pleasure Principle*, chapters 5 and 6. Freud links that instinct to the wish of inanimate things not to change, at a time in the beginning of the evolution of species that seems to fit the characteristics of the axolotls.

17. Describing the way "the great short story" expresses an obsessive presence which its author has to get rid of, Cortázar says that it was in such a state of mind that he wrote many of his stories, including some relatively long ones, like "The Secret Weapons." "The overpowering anguish that he felt through the course of an entire day, forced him to work without stopping until he finished the story and stopped being Pierre and Michèle" ("Del cuento breve y sus alrededores," in *Ultimo round* 1:59–72, at 68).

18. The narrator says that around 1928 (Cortázar was then fourteen years old) he went to the "Pasaje Güemes" in Buenos Aires (where there were prostitutes) in order to get rid of his childhood (*Todos los fuegos* 168).

19. Each of the two parts into which the story is divided is preceded by a quotation from *Les chants de Maldoror*. Once the protagonist is about to address the mysterious other Southamerican who is often in the same cafe that he frequents, but at the last minute decides not to. Alejandra Pizarnik ("Nota sobre un cuento de Julio Cortázar") sees the story as, among other things, a reenactment of Maldoror's struggle with his own shadow.

20. The gatherings of the prostitutes and their friends in the cafes allude to impressionist paintings, especially by Toulouse-Lautrec; the projected trip to the *moulin de la Butte*, to paintings by Renoir.

21. Included in *The Secret Weapons*. The bibliography on this novella is quite large. See especially Saúl Sosnowski, "Conocimiento poético."

22. For a thorough study of the psychological, and more specifically sexual implications of *Bestiario*, see Jaime Concha, "*Bestiario*, de Julio Cortázar."

23. In "Reunión," a story about the meeting of Che Guevara and Fidel Castro in the Sierra Maestra.

24. See the open letter of 1967 to Roberto Fernández Retamar, included under the title "Acerca de la situación del intelectual latinoamericano," in *Ultimo round*, vol. 2.

25. See Marta Paley de Francescato, "The New Man" in Alazraki and Ivask, *The Final Island* 134–39.

26. The preface to the story tells of how it was found by a member of Cortázar's family together with other papers of his. The author describes it as "a sort of *cuentecito* completely forgotten and very silly . . . Petulant, naive" (*La vuelta al día* 2:105).

27. "Del sentimiento de no estar del todo," in *La vuelta al día* 1:32–38, at 36. The same experience is mentioned in "Del sentimiento de lo fantástico," ibid., 69–75, at 70.

Chapter Four

The Fantastic in Contemporary Fiction

Borges and Cortázar Contrasted

The stories by Borges that make use of the supernatural and can thus appropriately be called fantastic are so only in a secondary kind of way, as I have tried to show. They function as metaphors of writing and the creative act in general ("The Aleph" being the most encompassing story in this regard, a true ars poetica), or as vehicles for speculation of a philosophical kind, or both.

With the notable exception of "There Are More Things," a terror tale the meaning of which is exhausted by the fear it provokes, Borges' "fantastic" *ficciones* can be said to be aimed at elaborating another text outside of the literal narrative. This meta-text, which is even more concise than its vehicle, the explicit narrative that we read, expresses the fundamental convictions that persistently occupy Borges. In summary, these consist of the following: the absolute universality of all ideas, with the equally absolute denial of originality as its corollary, and the affirmation of individuality as the sole truth regarding man's position in the world. The latter constitutes an apparent contradiction of the former concept, yet it does not contradict it within Borges' system. Since his most basic conviction is that real communication with our fellow beings is impossible (see Franco, "Utopia of a Tired Man"), individualism is actually strengthened by our isolation: we do not know that our neighbors' thoughts are interchangeable with our own. Meanwhile, the impossibility of communication among human beings results in making all intellectual endeavors useless.

These ideas are developed in both fantastic and non-fantastic stories in order to deal with specific concerns, such as the art of writing. Often Borges' decidedly didactic art looks for explicitly allegorical ways of developing precise expressions of his central convictions: e.g., the world is like a library made up of meaningless books and run by pure hazard, totally independent of human (i.e., individual, since men are always seen in isolation in Borges' *ficciones*) effort. Given the fact that most of those narratives are about something other than what the text suggests at the literal level, they could all be broadly categorized as allegorical. Borges' good reputation in academic circles attests to the subtlety and complexity with which his stories accomplish this reference outside of themselves to another reality. They never do this by simply subordinating the narrative to the concept embodied in it.

Cortázar has written several straightforward fantastic stories; and a good many of his stories, in addition, make full use of the most characteristic tools of the fantastic in ways that Borges' stories practically never do. In fact, at least a handful of Cortázar's best known and most justly famous narratives cannot be called anything but fantastic, since, even if positing the existence of the supernatural is not their primary aim, they provoke our hesitation regarding its presence and sometimes sustain that hesitation beyond the close of the narrative ("The Gates of Heaven" in particular). Some of Cortázar's fantastic stories, particularly those from *Bestiario*, come very close to Kafka's typical handling of the genre. They suggest a transcendental reality in a way that, at the same time, systematically eludes any attempt to identify or define that reality, thus postponing indefinitely the uncovering of the ultimate meaning of the story. This technique, the development of an elusive—because it has many possible meanings—allegory, differs substantially from the rather direct allegorical technique employed by Borges (as he himself acknowledges in the preface to *Ficciones*).

Cortázar tends toward the concrete much more than Borges, and as a born novelist deeply interested in human psychology and relationships, he is less prone than Borges to abstract speculation. This is what makes *Bestiario* such a puzzling book; the fantastic appears in many of its stories rooted in a solid psychological—and even physiological, as in "Cefalea"— reality of the type systematically avoided by Borges.

From the very beginning of Cortázar's career as a storyteller, his stories were not, although they employed the supernatural, really concerned with its presence, but rather with the imagination and with exploring the hidden aspects of man's relation with the world and other human beings. The vehicle through which that exploration is conducted is the unconscious, of course; its ultimate aim, to transcend reality. Because Cortázar's interest in that realm beyond the visible one and in the unconscious in general grew in the course of his career, he became less interested than other practitioners of the fantastic in painting the materialization of the supernatural the way he had done in the fantastic stories of *Bestiario*. He continued, however, to do this occasionally ("The Condemned Door," "Encounter with a Red Circle," "Text in a Notebook"), as he also continued to employ the fantastic, at times almost playfully, to develop other concerns. The texts cited above stop at the apparition of a supernatural passage into the unknown instead of probing into it like "The Idol of the Cyclades," "The Night Face Up," "Axolotl," "The Secret Weapons," "The Other Heaven," and, now pursuing the implications that the passage has for a reordering of society, "The Southern Highway," "Instructions for John Howell," and "Press Clippings." It can be stated that Cortázar was concerned all his life as an artist with searching for an almost mystic passage to states of consciousness capable of establishing communication with a time, a space, and even a species entirely different from the ordinary, except that through that contact a being which turns out to be an exact image of ourselves comes into existence.

Borges too is interested in that "other" who is also oneself; but his interest arises out of a very different concern. Contact with the double confirms Borges' characteristic belief in the identical nature of all experience, and by extension, of all subjects. This, in turn, serves as a philosophical justification for his even more basic belief in the absolute impossibility of communication between human beings. In turn, the sameness and repeatability of all experience make doubly useless any effort to reach out to the experiences of others.

Cortázar, for his part, is fully involved in trying to establish a link with that other being and the other world at the end of the passage. His is an active, existential search; he aims not at explaining but at identifying with his own other self living in another dimension. It should be stressed once more that the passage sought by Cortázar, although it belongs by definition to the realm of the irrational, is always placed in his stories within a strictly psychological framework. Nor is what awaits us at the other end of the passage less real than what we experience on this side, since the writer believes in its existence. That belief continued to the very end to be a generating force for Cortázar's art; however, by the time that the stories included in *All Fires the Fire* were written, it appears to have become less urgent or absorbing, suggesting that he thought that instead of appearing suddenly and arbitrarily, the passage could be actively sought

and even opened by the imagination. Cortázar would continue to explore
that opening in fantastic and non-fantastic stories throughout his career,
but he would also write stories that have very little or nothing to do with
it. Meanwhile in his later works, a new concern began to occupy Cortázar:
the need to define in his art a commitment to man's struggle for freedom—
in all dimensions, but most pointedly in a political sense.

That Cortázar has written more stories in the true spirit of the
fantastic than has Borges is, in the final account, the result of his relationship to reality, which he tries to capture in all its complexity especially
with regard to human relations. This does not mean, of course, that
Cortázar is, as a short story writer and novelist, a realist. Quite the
contrary, he is interested in depicting reality only in order to probe into
it in search of an access to another dimension, to what might be called a
supra-reality. That access, however, is pursued through reality itself,
without leaving out any of its components. It is precisely his interest in
reality that leads Cortázar to posit its disruption (just as Henry James did,
though in his case in order to focus attention on the psychic processes
through which reality is perceived) and eventual transcendence. The latter
aim links his work to that of some of the first practitioners of the fantastic,
like Poe, Hoffmann, or Nerval, whose romantic impulse to negate everyday reality did not pass, as Cortázar's had to, through the sieve of psychological realism.

But Cortázar's passionate involvement with reality works also in
another way, enhancing, by the attention that he pays to it, the contrast
between the quotidian and the supernatural on which the fantastic effect
is based. Consequently, it is Cortázar who, in the course of trying to
transcend a reality that he finds impoverished, writes "real" fantastic
stories, while Borges' conviction that man is incapable of moving beyond
his basic isolation fosters a belief in the solidity of the world that impris-
ons him.[1] In his "fantastic" stories, reality is denied only temporarily,
as a device for developing a meta- or super-text.

Magical Realism

There is a strong tendency in Latin American criticism to discuss under the rubric of "magical realism" all those works that employ fantasy as a device, including sometimes those that are more appropriately simply called fantastic. This critical practice originated in the argument that the magical realism movement, which was initially limited to the plastic arts, and more specifically to painting, was particularly appropriate for portraying the Latin American reality.[2] That reality, it has been argued, is itself "magical," partly because of the vastness, variety, and wilderness of the Latin American geography and the natural phenomena that affect it, but even more so because of the mythic mentality that remains dominant in that world.

We should distinguish carefully between *realismo mágico* proper and *lo real maravilloso*. As defined by Alejo Carpentier, the inventor of the term, in the preface to his 1949 novel *The Kingdom of This World*, the latter consists of the way the Latin American reality seems "magical." This is due to the rich reservoir of myth-making capability that remains in the American (but more so in the Latin American) mind as a consequence of the virgin landscape, the presence of the Indian and the black, and the mixture of races. These conditions, in turn, can elicit in Europeans, when faced with the Latin American nature, a capacity for giving up rational thinking and searching for the impossible.[3]

This marvelous quality in Latin American reality does not translate, in Carpentier's view, into a technique for portraying such a reality in literature. He expects instead that its magic nature will make itself evident spontaneously, through a realistic, even historically documented (as in *The Kingdom of This World*) narrative.[4] *Realismo mágico*, on the other hand, in its literary application, may or may not posit as its base the intrinsic "magic" of the reality in which the action of the novel or the short story takes place.[5]

Considered solely as an approach to storytelling characterized by mixing—as if they were of the same nature—reality and the supernatural, magical realism is an acceptable and even useful term. It is, at any rate, a critical category that, regardless of how inappropriate it might be in relation to its source, is likely to continue being used. We should not, however, confuse it with the fantastic, nor assume that it is equivalent to "Magischer Realismus."

In her study of magical realism Chanady distinguishes with rare insight between it and the fantastic. She begins by criticizing Todorov's concept of hesitation as "too restrictive" for defining the fantastic (*Magical Realism* 12). She thinks that the hesitation, being "a reaction on the part of the reader to textual indications" is a less satisfactory way to determine the presence of the fantastic than the "*antinomy*, or the simultaneous presence of two conflicting codes in the text," neither of which "can be accepted in the presence of the other," with the result that "the apparently supernatural phenomenon remains inexplicable" and "the confusion of the reader faced with two conflicting codes of reality is often maintained throughout most of the text" (ibid.). That is, it is not restricted to a single moment, as Todorov claims. It is also wrong to exclude from the fantastic those narratives which feature an "unambiguously supernatural" occurrence before which "there is no justification to hesitate between a logical and an irrational explanation" (11). The reader, argues Chanady, does not actually hesitate between the conflicting codes of the rational and the unreal: his reaction is the consequence of perceiving an "antinomy" between the code of nature, presupposed and accepted as a given, and that of the supernatural, which is rejected as being inconsistent with the former. While the fantastic depends on the problematization of that antinomy (which provokes our perplexity, confusion, or hesitation, as Chanady herself notes [12], even when this is not accompanied by the need to choose between codes), magical realism does not present the supernatural as "problematic," but presents it instead in ways that do not "disconcert" the reader, stressing, rather, the coherence of the two autonomous perspectives (24). This constitutes a truly illuminating explanation of magical realism, which Chanady considers to be a mode rather than a genre. Let us now see how and to what degree it differs from "Magischer Realismus."

The artists whose style was labelled "Magischer Realismus" (better known now than the German initiators of the movement are the Americans Edward Hopper, Grant Wood, and Andrew Wyeth) wanted "to portray the strange, the uncanny, the eerie and the dream-like—but not the fantastic—aspects of everyday reality" (Menton 13). They aimed at a "new objectivity," to be achieved through an "ultrasharp focus," smooth surfaces, the substitution for the typically expressionistic close-up approach of a combination of close and far views governed by a centripetal force, the use of miniaturism and naive techniques, and a certain coldness or effacement of expression (17–25). The critic Franz Roh, the author of the quasi-oxymoron "magical realism," intended to characterize the movement that he termed "post expressionism," saw something magic in the way the constant mobility of everything produces, ironically, permanent objects. What makes possible the perception of that magical quality of reality is a sort of synthesis between the two opposite poles (similar in their opposition and alternation to baroque and classical) of impressionism—the precise reproduction of the impression made by the natural world—and expressionism—the transformation of the latter by the artist's sensibility.

Magical realism in the arts represented a return to realism after expressionism and abstraction, in order to explore the hidden or "magical" elements of reality. (Such an exploration was, of course, directly linked to surrealism's interest in achieving a superior awareness of the sensory world precisely by liberating the imagination from the constraints of the "reality principle.")

The goal of the Spanish American writers that are usually called magic-realists (Carpentier in his first novels and some of his short stories, Asturias, Rulfo, and García Márquez, to name only the best known) was not really to depict the magic lying underneath everyday reality, and even less, to portray that reality objectively. These were the goals of the magic-realist painters, who tried to accomplish them by stressing the mimetic character of painting with regard to landscapes and the human figure, while at the same time giving their paintings a subjective mood (Wyeth's "Christina's World") or distancing their subject from the viewer by underlining certain of its features or removing from it elements that we would normally expect (such as an abundance of human figures in Hopper's "Early Sunday Morning"). (These devices are similar to the defamiliarization practiced by the Russian formalists.) Instead, the Spanish American writers associated with magical realism reproduce reality in schematic, lyrical, exaggerated, caricatured ways which facilitate the momentary but frequent suspension of the tenets of realistic representation so as to allow for the introduction of supernatural events (as happens so often in *One Hundred Years of Solitude*) or types of communication that would be impossible in a realistic narrative (in Rulfo's *Pedro Páramo*, the dead and the living talk freely among themselves). That suspension of realism's rules is not aimed, as in the marvelous—the type of fantastic fiction most similar to magical realism because of its unproblematized incorporation of the impossible—at making us accept the intrusion of the supernatural into our reality, but at portraying it as coexisting side-by-side with the ordinary in ways that make it not at all terrifying.

But what finally differentiates writers like Rulfo or García Márquez from the practitioners of the fantastic is that those works of theirs which are considered magico-realist present a very distinctive model of reality. Reality for them remains permanently open to transformation by an imagination of the mystic-mythic type, although such a transformation does not occur continuously; if this were the case they would be writing legends or fairy tales. Consequently, they do not construct their narratives, even though they are about realistic people and actions, in the traditional realistic manner, which requires great closeness to its subject, but instead, always from a certain distance. This is necessary in order to make the appearance of that other, non-realistic, or fantastic element possible. Neither the writer of fantastic stories—who needs a solid reality for the intrusion of the supernatural to have the desired effect—nor the magic-realist painters aim at distancing themselves from reality even temporarily.

(I prefer not to place Miguel Angel Asturias within the so-called magical realist movement, since what he does, mainly in *Corn Men* [1949], but also in at least the first two novels of his "Banana Trilogy" [*Strong Wind*, of 1950, and *The Green Pope*, 1954] is to introduce in the narrative Indian myths and legends.[6] He does this rather extensively in *Hombres de maíz*, but always as an actual part of a story that is, nevertheless, intrinsically realistic. Apart from what this technique might tell us about the myth-making capacity of Guatemalans and how it may affect non-Guatemalans, it is very different from the handling of the supernatural, whether in brief flashes or in more prolonged sequences, by García Márquez, Rulfo, and other authors who, like them, do deliberately weave into the plots of their narratives full-fledged legends—though, of course, those authors may at times use as the basis for their supernatural scenes universal or local myths and legends.

Carpentier, in his representations of reality, has never crossed the border between a rational, typically Western vision and a mythical one. In *The Kingdom of This World*, the narrator explains how Mackandal, contrary to what his followers thought, died at the stake.[7] In the story "Trip to the Seed," Carpentier narrates a man's life following an order contrary to the normal chronology; but this technique, devised, as is the arrangement of events in other stories of the same period ["The Road to Santiago," "The Fugitives"] to show certain oppositions and cyclical coincidences in human life, is an artistic technique, not a way of seeing the universe.)

The writers that have been labelled magic-realists are not looking for a dream element in a realistically portrayed world, as were the painters studied by Franz Roh. They want, instead, to narrate reality in ways that permit and even foster the inclusion of the supernatural or the merely uncanny, not as something in opposition to that reality, but as the materialization of unconscious processes or, in some cases, of man's capacity for myth-making.

A recent comment by the American novelist and critic John Updike stresses precisely the realistic basis of magical realism: "So-called 'magic realism' I take to be basically a method of nostalgia: the past—personal, familial, and national—weathers into fabulous shapes in memory without surrendering its fundamental truth. Fantasy, for García Márquez and his followers [Updike is reviewing a novel by Isabel Allende], is a higher level of honesty and directness in the rendering of experiences that have become subjectivized and mythologized" ("Resisting the Big Guys" 84).

Cortázar, on the other hand, does not weave the supernatural into the narrative's fabric (the tiger of "Bestiary") as just one more element of it, but gives it the prominence characteristic of the impossible in genuine fantastic stories. In other words, even when the supernatural is described as an accepted component of reality, it has an awesome quality that clearly distinguishes it from, and affects ordinary reality. Even though Cortázar does not stress the contradiction between the two antinomic codes of the real and the unreal, but blends one with the other in his description, as we saw again and again in *Bestiario*, the reader is made to feel that contradiction, and is asked to reject one or the other. This is not the case when we are told in *One Hundred Years of Solitude* that a girl flew to heaven or that the blood of a dying man went in search of his mother. We know when we read those descriptions that the author has playfully introduced a truly impossible, even supernatural element within reality merely in order to underline certain aspects of it (the veneration for purity, the strength of the ties between mother and son). But he does this through a peculiar perception of reality, linked to myths and dreams, and, more specifically, characteristic of the child's acceptance of the possibility of the impossible happening in his everyday life, just as it does in the stories told or read to him. That approach is in fact so unique that it constitutes an individual style. When encountered in other writers, it seems derivative.

At the same time, Cortázar's search for a passage between reality and the oneiric, and his claim that the two are connected, links his work with the magic-realist painters' wish to unveil the uncanny element hidden in ordinary reality. But while they pursued that aim by stressing the reality of the world's surface until it showed what we normally fail to perceive in it, Cortázar does so by bringing to the foreground the supernatural.

For his part, Borges does not strive in his stories for a super objective portrait of reality (realistic detail and psychological characterization being for him only accessory to achieving certain goals); nor does he seem interested in the eerie underside of reality. Borges' introduction of the supernatural and the impossible is, as we have seen, almost always the vehicle for developing meditations distinct from the portrayal of reality and the exploration of its uncanny qualities. It is true, at the same time, that stories like "The Shape of the Sword," "The Garden of Forking Paths," or "The South," which sometimes evoke the fantastic by slightly distorting reality, or by introducing strange happenings and improbable coincidences, may remind the reader of the techniques employed by the so-called "magico-realist" writers. Those and similar stories remain, however, truly non-fantastic regardless of how much they may bewilder us.[8] It is thus confusing to link them to the work of writers such as García Márquez, whose use of the fantastic aims at opening up a realistic account to myth-making possibilities (of the type peculiar to fairy tales), or with that of Rulfo, who employs the supernatural for the very specific purpose of making the spirits of the dead communicate with each other.

The Role of the Fantastic

In his 1947 article on Blanchot and Kafka "Aminadab ou du fantastique considerée comme une langage," Sartre discusses the art of those writers as an example of the last stage of fantastic literature. It is no longer necessary in contemporary manifestations of the fantastic to bring in, in order to achieve the fantastic effect, the supernatural or even the extraordinary, says Sartre, since often what is accepted as normal in our world is actually quite uncanny. In fact, it appears at times as if we no longer knew the meaning of our own actions or the true function and reason of the objects that we constantly use without paying real attention to them. Kafka reveals, by looking at it from the outside, that we all inhabit a truly fantastic world without being aware of it. Blanchot uses the same technique, except that in his case there is no longer any belief in transcendence, which Kafka, on the other hand, still aims for, although recognizing that it is unreachable.

These comments suggest the disappearance of the fantastic as a genre. What characterizes, or at least what used to characterize the fantastic, the portrayal of the supernatural, is no longer needed in order to call attention to the true strangeness of a world that seems capable of absorbing even the most unusual occurrences. At the same time, Sartre's reflections point to a drastic extension of the fantastic beyond its traditional boundaries, a generalization of its presence and effects that would fit the definitions of the fantastic by some of the critics discussed in the first section of this study.

Maurice Blanchot, one of the pioneer voices of post-modernism, and an author whose work Sartre thought was an expression of the "new fantastic," has argued against the notion of genre in contemporary literature. For Blanchot there is no longer an intermediary—i.e., the structure of a genre—between the individual text and literature as a whole. And this, the ultimate genre, is the very thing that every modern work questions (see *Le livre à venir*). Blanchot's denial of the existence of genres supports from a theoretical standpoint the arguments in favor of extending until they are actually eliminated the limits that define the fantastic as a genre primarily concerned with provoking a hesitation in the reader in the face of the supernatural.

Taking as his point of departure Blanchot's statements regarding the subject, Todorov has investigated the notion of literary genre (see "The Origin of Genres"), demonstrating that our sense of genre as a class of texts which has been perceived as such throughout the course of history corresponds to a reality that projects itself into certain horizons of expectation for readers and into definite models of writing. The genre is the point of intersection of general poetics (which points to the existence of modes and styles not fixed in time, and generally available to all speakers) and literary history (schools and movements that attest, historically, to certain codifications of discursive properties). Genres coincide with and codify some speech acts that were originally non-literary. Todorov proves this by showing how the fantastic—codified as the subject "I" plus a verb of attitude and the modalization of that verb in the direction of uncertainty, plus a subordinate clause describing a supernatural event—is found outside written literature, specifically in the African *luba*, a type of invitation which is then enriched in writing through narrativization, gradation, and thematic proliferation. The fantastic as genre, concludes Todorov, encodes an empirical property of the discursive act which is also found outside written literature.

It follows from this that the possibility for the fantastic to develop as a genre exists always within man's interest in the supernatural, which is, of course, a manifestation of a basic uncertainty regarding his position in the universe. It could be argued then that the literature whose aim is to express man's relationship to that which, because it lies beyond his comprehension, threatens him, should be considered a mode, i.e., an artistically controlled way of expressing, of channeling a *fantasy* in the direction of representing the supernatural. That mode comprises, together with all literary embodiments of the supernatural, the various expressions of the fantastic described by Todorov, from the fantastic uncanny to science fiction and the fairy tale (except that the latter fits also, even more obviously so than science fiction, within the romance considered as a mode).

The fantastic mode includes the fantastic proper. This I will now attempt to define, basically following Todorov, but trying at the same time, as the observations of some critics (Chanady, Brooke-Rose, Cixous, etc.) suggest, to broaden the parameters of Todorov's definition of the fantastic to allow the actual practice of the genre to fit more comfortably into that definition. The fantastic is a type of narrative that portrays the existence within a strictly realistic milieu (either as a sudden intrusion or as something that was there already at the beginning of the story) of a supernatural or impossible—and not merely extraordinary, strange, or uncanny—element. The requirement for a realistic setting excludes from the fantastic traditional allegorical literature, which clearly uses the supernatural for no other purpose than to convey its message. Excluded also from the fantastic are narratives like fairy tales, which, though directed by different aims, take place in a world totally removed from ordinary reality. Nor does the occasional use of the supernatural for purposes that vary from changing the rhythm of a narrative to stating something that can best be said through it suffice to qualify a work as fantastic. In other words, the fantastic demands that our notion of what is possible be deliberately challenged in more or less forceful ways by an element that appears to exist next to, yet in direct opposition to the quotidian world. The presence of that element provokes a hesitation in the reader as to the possibility of its being real and thus acceptable. This is due to the fact that the spirit of the realistic environment surrounds the supernatural element, prompting us to accept it. However, this hesitation is exclusively dependent on the way the narrative is developed; it is provoked only by focusing on the supernatural element in a way that underlines the contrast between it and its realistic milieu. If that contrast is ignored, the fantastic element— because we must still deal with it as long as the presence of the supernatural is given any prominence against the background reality—calls for immediate acceptance without the intrusion of any uncertainty.

The duration of the hesitation depends directly on the relative believability of the event portrayed. It may be deepened and prolonged by insisting on the event's reality no matter how intrinsically unbelievable it is; but its importance can also be drastically diminished by not giving it explicit expression through one of the characters in the story or through the authorial voice. The hesitation may also be left unresolved at the end, so that it turns into a long-lasting doubt; or it may be closed by accepting the supernatural or, going in the opposite direction, by producing an ostensibly natural explanation of the phenomenon in question. (This solution, typical of Poe, is rare in contemporary literature, due to the universal increase in scientific knowledge and the consequent reduction in readers' susceptibility to obviously fake scientific explanations.) Although the reader may have decided from the start to reject the possibility that the extraordinary event or presence could be real, inasmuch as he has entered a contract with the writer that compels him to accept as "real" the elements of the narrative, he must continue to consider the supernatural element, no matter how impossible, a reality.

What in the final account makes a text fantastic is that an obviously impossible event takes place in and is contrasted with a thoroughly realistic environment. It does not matter ultimately that the only justification for the supernatural occurrence, regardless of whether this is clearly expressed ("Funes," "Pierre Menard," "The Southern Thruway") or remains mute (the *Bestiario* stories) is meta-literary or allegorical. The fantastic depends for its existence and its effect not on the interpretation of its implications, but on the contradiction that it creates between the possible and the impossible.

This *genre*, as an analysis of stories by Borges and Cortázar confirms, seems very much alive. To call, as did Sartre, for extending the notion of the fantastic to the whole of modern (Kafka) and postmodern (Blanchot) literature, as expressive of a reality that, especially since World War II, has itself turned "fantastic," ignores the fact that contemporary literature continues to represent the supernatural as a phenomenon that requires an explanation. At the same time, that the fantastic developed as a literary genre from a certain type of speech act reflecting a basic attitude of uncertainty before the supernatural, does not imply that it will persist forever in all cultures untouched by the social circumstances that make genres wane and disappear. Even though the cell of meaning from which the fantastic sprang may be found in every culture, and even though it is still active in ours, its formalization in the genre called "the fantastic" not only can be but is very likely to be affected by the passage of historical time.

Bellemin-Nöel restates Todorov's assertion that the death of the fantastic is tied to what he refers to in his essay as "the widening of the Freudian breach (*coupure*)" ("Des formes fantastiques" 118). The genre formerly expressed the unconscious processes through which man faced the dark forces working against him, and which rational thought tried to ignore until the Freudian revolution. The expression of the unconscious was first triggered and then actively fostered by romanticism. Since then, literature has expressed man's most intimate desires not only through the mediation of what Freud would call the reality principle, but also at another level, at which those desires are basically unconscious of themselves and of their own implications, mainly because these involve the most secret layers of the subject's psyche. It is then that desires—and the fears that constitute their other side—often take on the shape of a supernatural intrusion—a supernatural intrusion which is problematized through a narrative that questions its very possibility. The other type of representation of the supernatural, "naive" and non-questioning, was already practiced before romanticism made us half aware of unconscious states. And it has continued to be practiced after the development of psychoanalytical theory in the twentieth century in fairy tale-type narratives (such as Tolkien's) and in science fiction. As they did in other times, such texts still serve to give expression to our fears and desires.

(It does not follow from this, however, as Bellemin-Nöel asserts, that science fiction has taken over the fantastic's mission of expressing a "troubled sensitivity" as well as the oneiric, while the fantastic itself has disappeared into "the general problematic of writing after the revolutions of Proust, Joyce, and surrealism" [118]. Science fiction's approach to the impossible is basically unproblematic. This, the direct result of the portrayal by science fiction literature of the referential world not as a complex reality, but as the impossible accepted, makes science fiction a mass public-oriented genre, as Bellemin-Nöel himself says [ibid.], and hardly a suitable vehicle for expressing the oneiric or any of the problems related to an estranged, alienated sensibility.)

The contemporary practice of the fantastic is carried out with very different goals and often in strikingly different forms from the ones that characterized the genre in the nineteenth century, that is, before Freud pulled away the veil concealing the fears and desires of the young governess in *The Turn of the Screw*. The fantastic after Freud changed direction as a literary vehicle. It seems certain, judging from those examples of the genre by Poe, Hoffmann, Villiers de l'Isle-Adam, Merimée, Maupassant, and Henry James studied by Todorov as well as other critics, that the fantastic evolved mainly as a way of expressing the unconscious forces that the liberation of spiritual energy facilitated by romanticism had prompted artists to respond to. By the end of the nineteenth century, the fantastic, which was by then a full-fledged genre within the literary representation of the supernatural, had developed its link to the unconscious into a formula—the supernatural enters a solid reality, provoking the hesitation of the characters or merely of the reader—that continues to be used outside and beyond the connection with the unconscious. In fact, the contemporary fantastic rarely represents that connection in a raw, unmediated form.

When Cortázar says that fantastic stories are "neurotic products," he is pointing to a self-awareness that is intrinsically alien to Poe's fantastic stories, for instance. This is precisely what makes the obviously "neu-

rotic" stories of *Bestiario* so difficult to explain; some sort of consciousness of what they are really about functions as a mediator between their
source in the writer's subconscious and other levels and possibilities of
meaning, some of which are allegorical. Cortázar also talks about "neu-
tralizing" those "nightmares" or "hallucinations," and, in a slightly
different context, of "exorcising" the "invading creatures," all of which
underlines the presence of a knowledge, no matter how complete, of their
intimate meaning for the writer himself. As the modern artist has become
increasingly aware of his own psychological processes, he is less and less
likely to employ the fantastic to recreate them, especially since the forces,
biological as well as social, that the supernatural had embodied can now
be given full expression in realistic garb. It seems, at the same time, that
Cortázar's use of the fantastic decreased in proportion to the increase in
his knowledge of his own unconscious, a self-knowledge that changes the
"neurotic" presences and anguished passages of *Bestiario* into the ease
with which the "passage" is sought in "The Other Heaven." In the final
account, the unconscious is a very broad concept, capable of including,
in addition to the strictly subconscious mind mediated by the writer's
consciousness, the way the former interprets social reality (see Jameson,
Political Unconscious).

The codification of the fantastic into generic devices which is the
consequence of its development into a genre results in facilitating its use
for other purposes without having to renounce its nature. In both Borges'
and Cortázar's fantastic stories, the supernatural is used for developing
allegories, for commenting on literature and on the self, for evoking
contacts between the real and the oneiric, and, specifically in the case of
the latter, for opening a passage into another reality or level of consciousness, a task for which the fantastic is particularly well suited. These objec-
tives differ substantially from the evocation of private ghosts on which the
traditional fantastic was intent.

The stories by Borges and Cortázar that exemplify the continuation
of the fantastic in contemporary literature (as opposed to the ones that are
basically allegorical or oneiric) include the supernatural as a more or less
disturbing presence within an otherwise realistic setting, and consequently,
force us as readers to question, however briefly, that presence or element.
The introduction of an impossible element within a realistic story is
normally achieved in those narratives through different, more complex
means—by paying close attention to psychological detail (Cortázar) or by
developing the philosophical implications of the supernatural element
(Borges)—from those typical of the classical fantastic. Sometimes the nar-

rator's reliability is made suspect in order to counteract the forcefulness of the presence of the supernatural. Often the impossible is affirmed from the very beginning of the story to the forceful exclusion of all doubt regarding its existence.

It is obvious, at the same time, that the contemporary fantastic, as exemplified not only in the work of Borges and Cortázar, but also in that of other writers who use some of the tools of the genre (specifically, the impossible) to varying degrees, such as Tomasso Landolfi, Dino Buzzatti, Italo Calvino, or Thomas Pynchon,[9] shows a definite tendency toward developing a super-text of some kind, for which the actual narrative functions as a basis, without, however, being always subordinated to it as in straight allegories and thesis-directed fiction. That super-text serves in the post-Kafka fantastic the same function as the representation of the unconscious did in previous manifestations of the genre. It points to another meaning, also partially hidden; but in contemporary fiction this is very often associated with universal propositions and with "truths" of more limited scope having to do with literature, the self, other dimensions of consciousness. But the impossible can be so opaque to meaning, while still being very concrete, that it leads to an interpretative dead end by fostering the multiplication of interpretations.

It might be useful in this respect to take a brief look at a text by an American writer who is considered to be postmodern. In Thomas Pynchon's *The Crying of Lot 49* (1966), a woman who has been named executor of the estate of a former boyfriend uncovers in the course of her legal inquiries the existence of what appears to be a vast and utterly mysterious conspiracy. Its goal, dating back to the beginning of the modern era in the sixteenth century, and involving spying and murder, seems to be to distribute mail independently of the government-operated postal service. *The Crying* is structured like a detective novel, something which fulfills Borges' ideal equation of the fantastic with the action-dominated plot in which psychological characterization is secondary. But Pynchon's novel is also allegorical in a manner that almost becomes explicit at the end.

Against the background of southern California's (the quintessential contemporary America) physical and moral landscape, while searching for the source of the clues that repeatedly come across her path but then evade her, Oedipa Maas, the former lover of Inverarity, feels increasingly burdened by the emptiness that surrounds her. As the executor of the mysterious Inverarity's ubiquitous and impossible-to-assess estate, the protagonist has become heiress to and also possibly manager of a legacy of silence, fear, and waste, which she finally perceives as representing the broken promise of which her country has become the image. When Oedipa finally realizes this, she feels pregnant with meaning, about to decipher and reveal a message. Her mission is precisely to act as intermediary between her old lover and those who await his message, the customers of the underground mail service for the unbalanced, the alienated, the oppressed, which is what the millions cut off from communicating with their fellow human beings have become. This is clearly a message about, if not a revolution, at least the need for a counterculture capable of turning the tide of massive selfish consumerism that is drowning the country—a feeling that was widespread at the time *The Crying* appeared.[10]

But when the existence of the conspiracy is about to be confirmed, thus making explicit the meaning of the novel, the action stops, as the lot of stamps that holds the secret to the mail service that Inverarity was involved with, is about to be "cried" at an auction. Will there be a bidder representing the conspiracy, as Oedipa has been led to believe? Is there in fact a plot that would confirm the reality of all those strange, often unbelievable events that the protagonist has construed to be clues leading to a secret that is, however, never uncovered? Our hesitation is carried to the very end of the text and even beyond it, in an open ending that suspends the spelling out of *The Crying*'s allegorical meaning to stress instead the fantastic aspect of the story.

This novel fits comfortably within Todorov's definition of the fantastic: the occurrence of a series of extremely uncanny events suggests a supernatural presence behind what seems to be a human conspiracy, except that it is too huge, too preposterous to be accepted. But the doubt is never cleared, thus leaving open the possibility of affirming the existence of the supernatural in view of the absence of the confirmation that everything was in fact planned by human beings. *The Crying* is, nevertheless, an allegorical work, and not of the type, typical of Kafka's handling of allegory, that constantly evades definition. Strangely enough, and contrary to what happens in traditional allegorical literature, the explication of the allegorical meaning does not in this case destroy the doubt created by the contrast between the impossible events that are its vehicle, and the reality. The same is true, as we saw, of several of Cortázar's stories.

The Crying's position between the fantastic and allegorical codes confirms outside the Hispanic world (but, of course, Borges' and Cortázar's works reflect contemporary literary trends as much as they have generated them) the capacity of the fantastic to embrace allegory without ceasing to problematize reality through the intervention of the supernatural. Pynchon's second novel also suggests that the fantastic tends naturally towards allegory (see Todorov,

Poetics 156), as is well illustrated also by Borges' and Cortázar's use of the supernatural to develop rather straight allegories. The commentary on literature and—in the case of Cortázar—the search for a passage through time and space are aims structurally akin to allegory, since they involve the development of a super-text encoded in the one explicitly developed by the narrative.

The immediacy of the super-text appears to be in exact but inverse proportion to the importance of the hesitation provoked by the intrusion of the supernatural. When that intrusion is not simply assumed as a given, but is capable of stirring doubts in the reader through the way the narrative contrasts it with a realistic setting, we are likely to become involved, at least for some time, with the presence of the supernatural, instead of directing all our efforts from the beginning to deciphering the meaning of the story. This is what happens in most of Cortázar's stories, but also in some of Borges' ("Funes," and even "Pierre Menard"), although in most of his fantastic *ficciones* the supernatural—which may make its appearance only at the end (as in "Tlön")—is obviously an instrument for elaborating a reflection on any of a variety of issues and as such it stirs hardly any hesitation in us. In narratives like "The God's Script" and "The Circular Ruins," the unreality of the setting against which the supernatural appears immediately directs our critical sense to look for the super-text that constitutes the purpose of the story. On the other hand, to develop the presence of the impossible element in conflict with the realistic data surrounding it (which denies its reality yet at the same time suggests that it might, after all, be possible) ends up strengthening the overall verisimilitude of the story. And realism, by its characteristic openness to a variety of uses, opposes the fixed limits of allegorical or other types of super-textual interpretations—which is what makes many of Kafka's narratives so difficult to interpret. In a story like "Bestiary," for example, the continuous presence of a peculiarly concrete type of supernatural element within a thoroughly realistic setting acts to prevent, although the narrative stubbornly ignores any kind of hesitation as to the reality of the tiger, the clear development of an allegorical meaning. It does this by focusing the reader's attention on the *factual* presence of the supernatural.

This near impossibility of determining the meaning of the story, accomplished relatively frequently by Cortázar, is, in conclusion, what best expresses the aim of the fantastic genre since its inception. The fantastic wishes to reproduce processes that are, by their very nature, being rooted in the unconscious, elusive. Thus, they remain hidden behind their transformation into supernatural presences. Furthermore, the fantastic narrative is itself only half aware at best of being a vehicle for the expression of what lies underneath consciousness. These two factors unite to produce a basic indeterminacy regarding meaning, just as in the best of Cortázar's fantastic stories, the conflicting codes of the supernatural and the realistic, in their constant clash, distract our attention from the super-text which is, at the same time, constantly being alluded to.

The continuing presence of the genre today, in forms that extend it beyond the role that the supernatural originally played in literature, is the consequence of its having embraced new goals, new possibilities for meaning that end up stressing its natural tendency—what we might call an ontological aspiration toward allegory and the development of a super-text. This is the result, ultimately, of operating from a non-realistic basis. It remains to be explained, however, why it is that writers like Borges, Cortázar, or Pynchon would choose the fantastic—i.e., the inclusion of the supernatural—in order to develop a super-text of varying purposes and depths. The reason might be that in the modern world, asserting a truth of some sort is best achieved through the vehicle of the supernatural, precisely because, since we no longer believe in the possibility of its presence, the supernatural functions as a kind of disclaimer of the statement made by the super-text.

As Fredric Jameson has explained, the search of the romance for equivalences of magic—"for reinventing the sacred" ("Magical Narratives" 145)—having run its course, the literature that we call "fantastic" seeks to convey the sacred, not as a presence, but rather as a determinate, marked absence at the heart of the secular world" (ibid.). The end product is a world "forever suspended on the point of meaning" (146) (which is how Borges in 1950 defined the artistic effect),[11] forever disposed to receive a revelation that never takes place, because in the secularized and alienated world of modern capitalism, epiphanies—the appearance of a supernatural (sacred) order guaranteeing the possibility of restoring an utopian world—are impossible; and we know this. That impossibility is expressed in the way the supernatural is developed in the modern fantastic against the background of a reality depicted since Hoffmann with increasing sophistication and psychological accuracy, so as to affirm the presence of the supernatural while at the same time making it more difficult to accept. The higher order alluded to by the story is thus negated and indirectly portrayed as an absence. The imagination that envisioned the community created by the traffic jam in the *autoroute du Sud*, Menard's *Don Quixote*, or a planet on which physical reality obeys the mind, is permanently kept in check by a world that accepts as valid only the vision of itself confirmed by empirical reality. This is precisely why, because it is well aware of that fact, the imagination chooses as its vehicle (or weapon) the supernatural, i.e., a total, and as such impossible breach of reality. This allows the artist's mind, at the same time, to affirm its capacity to create whatever images of itself it thinks fit to represent its powers and its fears before a world that refuses to believe, for example, that the meaning that the idol of the Cyclades had for its original worshippers can be restored in contemporary Paris.

In "The Aleph," Borges the realist accepts the destruction of the magic window on the universe by the developers that tear down Danieri's house, but saves it nevertheless from the ruthless machinery of capitalistic modernization by pulling away its *real* meaning from the magic that had erroneously enveloped it, explaining it instead as the artistic imagination. Cortázar, on the other hand, as witnessed by a story as late as "Press Clippings," insists on holding open a supernatural access to a world in which the imagination can be totally free to move beyond normal temporal and spatial limits.

Notes

1. At the end of his ambitious essay, "A New Refutation of Time" (in many ways a rewriting of the 1936 essay, "History of Eternity") included in *Other Inquisitions*, Borges says: "And yet, and yet [in English in the original]—To deny temporal succession, to deny the ego, to deny the astronomical universe, are apparent desperations and secret assuagements. Our destiny (unlike the hell of Swedenborg and the hell of Tibetan mythology) is not horrible because of its unreality; it is horrible because it is irreversible and ironbound" (*Other Inquisitions* 186).

2. See Franz Roh's 1925 *Nach-expressionismus, magischer realismus: Probleme der neusten europäischer Malerei*, translated into Spanish as *Realismo mágico: Post experesionismo: Problemas de la pintura europea más reciente*, with a reproduction, facing the title page, of Rousseau's painting, "Sleeper." Rousseau's neoprimitivism fits better within Roh's definition of expressionism than of postexpressionism, which in his view opposed to the "primitive and spontaneous," characteristic of expressionism, the "refined and professionally artistic." Roh dropped this contrast later, probably because he recognized the importance of Rousseau's technique for magic realism (see Menton, *Magic Realism Rediscovered* 17–18). Already by 1925, magic realist painting was being called "new objectivity" (at a show in Manheim), and Roh himself used that term in a 1958 book. A 1943 show at the New York Museum of Modern Art was called, on the other hand, "American Realists and Magic Realists."

3. In his preface, Roh makes a distinction between "magical" and "mythical." He opposed the former to the latter, he says, to "indicate that the mystery does not descend to the world represented [in the work of art] but hides and breathes behind it" (I quote from the Spanish edition). It can be argued, however, that a myth-oriented mind discovers the myths hidden behind ordinary reality.

4. *El reino*, Prólogo, 5–11. On Carpentier and magic realism, see Echevarría, "Isla a su vuelo fugitiva" 145–78. On the connections of Carpentier's *real maravilloso* and surrealism, see Angel Rama, "Los productivos años" 230–36.

5. García Márquez sees Latin American reality as, if not exactly "magic," at least so extraordinary that it often appears supernatural. He mentions several unbelievable events in his interviews with Plinio A. Mendoza, *El olor* (49–51).

6. Asturias' first book was a compilation of legends, *Leyendas de Guatemala* (1930). Prior to that he had translated into Spanish the *Popol Vuh* and the *Annals of the Cakchiquels*.

7. Mackandal manages indeed to free himself from the cords fastening him to the stake and to "fly" towards the slaves witnessing the execution. The omniscient narrator then explains that the ensuing commotion was such that "very few saw that Mackandal, held by the soldiers, was placed on the fire and that a flame, increased by the burning hair, swallowed his last cry" (*El reino* 41).

8. For a different opinion, see Menton, "Jorge Luis Borges, Magic Realist."

9. I am referring to some of the stories included in Landolfi's collection *Gogol's Wife* and to his novella *Cancerqueen*; to Buzatti's novel *The Tartar Steppe*; to Calvino's novels *The Nonexistent Knight*, *The Cloven Viscount*, and *The Baron in the Trees*, as well as to the stories included in his *Cosmicomics* and the first part of *T Zero*; and to Pynchon's *The Crying of Lot 49*.

10. See Charles A. Reich, *Greening of America*.

11. "Music, states of happiness, mythology, faces molded by time, certain twilights and certain places—all these are trying to tell us something, or have told us something we should not have missed, or are about to tell us something; that imminence of a revelation that is not yet produced is, perhaps, the aesthetic reality" (*Other Inquisitions* 5).

Works Cited

Alazraki, Jaime. *En busca del unicornio: Los cuentas de Julio Cortázar.* Madrid: Gredos, 1983.

——. *La prosa narrativa de Jorge Luis Borges.* Madrid: Gredos, 1974.

——, and Ivan Ivask, eds. *The Final Island: The Fiction of Julio Cortázar.* Norman: Univ. of Oklahoma Press, 1978.

Anderson Imbert, Enrique. "Un cuento de Borges: 'La casa de Asterión.' " *Revista iberoamericana* 26.49 (1960): 33–43.

Barrenechea, Ana María. "Ensayo de una tipología de la literatura fantástica." *Revista iberoamericana* 38.80 (1972): 391–403.

——. "La literatura fantástica: Función de los códigos socioculturales en la constitución de un género." In *Texto/contexto en la literatura iberoamericana*, Memoria del XIX Congreso del Instituto internacional de literatura iberoamericana, 1979. Madrid: IILI, 1981. 11–19.

Bellemin-Noël, Jean. "Des formes fantastiques aux thèmes fantasmatiques." *Littérature* 2 (May 1971): 103–28.

Bessière, Irene. *Le récit fantastique.* Paris: Larousse, 1974.

Bioy Casares, Adolfo. *La invención de Morel.* Buenos Aires: Emecé, 1968.

Blanchot, Maurice. "L'infini littéraire: L'*Aleph.*" In *Le livre à venir.* Paris: Gallimard, 1959.

——. *Le livre à venir.* Paris: Gallimard, 1959.

Borges, Jorge Luis. *El aleph.* Buenos Aires: Emecé, 1957.

——. *The Aleph and Other Stories: 1939–1940.* Ed. and trans. Norman Thomas di Giovanni. New York: E. P. Dutton, 1978.

———. "El arte narrativo y la magia." In *Discusión*. Madrid: Alianza Editorial, 1976. 71–79.

———. *The Book of Sand*. Trans. Norman Thomas di Giovanni. New York: E. P. Dutton, 1978.

———. *Cartas de juventud (1921–1922)*. Ed. Carlos Meneses. Madrid: Orígenes, 1987.

———. *Discusión*. Madrid: Alianza Editorial, 1976.

———. *Dr. Brodie's Report*. Trans. Norman Thomas di Giovanni. New York: E. P. Dutton, 1978.

———. *Ficciones*. Buenos Aires: Emecé, 1958.

———. *El informe de Brodie*. Buenos Aires: Emecé, 1972.

———. *El libro de arena*. Buenos Aires: Emecé, 1975.

———. *Other Inquisitions*. Trans. Ruth L. C. Simms. Austin and London: Univ. of Texas Press, 1964.

Brandt Rojas, José H. "Asedios a 'Casa tomada.'" *Revista de estudios hispánicos* (Univ. of Puerto Rico) 7 (1980): 75–84.

Brooke-Rose, Christine. "Historical Genres/Theoretical Genres: A Discussion of Todorov on the Fantastic." *New Literary History* 8.1 (1976): 145–58. (Also included in her *Rhetoric of the Unreal*.)

———. *A Rhetoric of the Unreal: Studies in Narrative and Structure, Especially of the Fantastic*. Cambridge: Cambridge Univ. Press, 1981.

Carpentier, Alejo. *El reino de este mundo*. Havana: Letras Cubanas, 1984.

Chanady, Amaryll Beatrice. *Magical Realism and the Fantastic: Resolved Versus Unresolved Antinomy*. New York and London: Garland, 1985.

Christ, Ronald. *The Narrow Act: Borges' Art of Allusion*. New York: New York Univ. Press, 1961.

Cixous, Hélène. "La fiction et ses fantômes: Une lecture de l'*Unheimliche* de Freud." In *Prénoms de personne*. Paris: Seuil, 1974.

Concha, Jaime. "*Bestiario*, de Julio Cortázar, o el tigre en la biblioteca." *Hispamérica* 11.32 (1982): 3–21.

Cortázar, Julio. "Algunos aspectos del cuento." In *Literatura y arte nuevo en cuba*. Barcelona: Estela, 1971. 261–76.

———. *Bestiario*. Buenos Aires: Sudamericana, 1969.

———. *Ceremonias*. Barcelona: Seix Barral/Nueva Narrativa Hispánica, 1968.

———. *Libro de Manuel*. Buenos Aires: Sudamericana, 1973.

———. *Queremos tanto a Glenda*. Madrid: Alfaguara, 1983.

———. *Los relatos*. Madrid: Alianza Editorial, 1976.

———. *Todos los fuegos el fuego*. Buenos Aires: Sudamericana, 1970.

——. *Ultimo round*. 2 vols. Madrid: Siglo XXI, 1972.

——. *La vuelta al día en ochenta mundos*. 2 vols. Madrid: Siglo XXI, 1978.

Culler, Jonathan. "Literary Fantasy." *Cambridge Review* 23 (Nov. 1973): 30–33.

Derrida, Jacques. *La dissémination*. Paris: Seuil, 1972.

Franco, Jean. "Utopia of a Tired Man: Jorge Luis Borges." *Social Text* 4 (Fall 1981): 52–78.

Freud, Sigmund. *Beyond the Pleasure Principle. The Standard Edition of the Complete Psychological Works of Sigmund Freud*. Trans. James Strachey. London: Hogarth, 1966.

García Márquez, Gabriel. *El olor de la quayaba*. Barcelona: Bruguera, 1983.

Genette, Gérard. "La littérature selon Borges." *L'Herne* (1964): 323–27.

——. "L'utopie littéraire." In *Figures*. Paris: Seuil, 1966.

González Echevarría, Roberto. "Isla a su vuelo fugitiva." In *Isla a su vuelo fugitiva: Ensayos críticos sobre literatura hispanoamericana*. Madrid: Porrúa Turanzas, 1983. 155–57.

Holquist, Michael. "Whodunit and Other Questions: Metaphysical Detective Stories in Post-War Fiction." *New Literary History* 3.1 (1971): 135–56.

Irby, James E. "Borges and the Idea of Utopia." In *The Cardinal Points of Borges*. Ed. Lowell Dunham and Ivan Ivask. Norman: Univ. of Oklahoma Press, 1971. 35–45.

Irwin, W. I. *The Game of the Impossible: A Rhetoric of Fantasy*. Urbana: Univ. of Illinois Press, 1976.

Jackson, Rosemary. *Fantasy: The Literature of Subversion*. London and New York: Methuen, 1981.

Jameson, Fredric. "Magical Narratives: Romance as Genre." *New Literary History* 7.1 (1975): 135–63. A version of this essay is included in Jameson's *The Political Unconscious*.

——. *The Political Unconscious: Narrative as a Socially Symbolic Act*. Ithaca: Cornell Univ. Press., 1981.

Jitrik, Noé. "Notas sobre la 'zona sagrada' y el mundo de los 'otros' en *Bestiario*." In *La vuelta a Cortázar en nueve ensayos*, ed. Noé Jitrik. Buenos Aires: Carlos Pérez Editor, 1968. 13–30.

Menton, Seymour. "Jorge Luis Borges, Magic Realist." *Hispanic Review* 50 (1982): 411–26.

——. *Magic Realism Rediscovered*. Philadelphia: The Art Alliance Press; London and Toronto: Associated Univ. Presses, 1983.

Morello-Frosch, Marta. " 'La banda' de los otros: Política fantástica en un cuento de Julio Cortázar." In *Homenaje a Ana María Barrenechea*. Ed. Lía Schwartz Lerner and Isaías Lerner. Madrid: Castalia, 1984. 497–503.

Mundo Lo, Sara de. *Julio Cortázar: His Work and His Critics: A Bibliography*. Urbana: Albatross, 1985.

Ortega, Julio. "La dinámica de lo fantástico en 4 cuentos de Cortázar." *Revista de crítica literaria latinoamericana* 11.23 (1986): 127–34.

Picón Garfield, Evelyn. *Julio Cortázar*. New York: Frederick Ungar, 1975.

Pizarnik, Alejandra. "Nota sobre un cuento de Julio Cortázar: 'El otro cielo.'" In *La vuelta a Cortázar en nueve ensayos*. Ed. Noé Jitrik, Buenos Aires: Carlos Pérez Editor, 1968. 55–62.

Planells, Antonio. "'Casa tomada' o la parábola del limbo." *Revista iberoamericana* 52.135–36 (1986): 591–603.

Rabkin, Eric. *The Fantastic in Literature*. Princeton: Princeton Univ. Press, 1976.

Rama, Angel. "Los Productivos años setenta de Alejo Carpentier (1904–1980)." *Latin American Research Review* 16.2 (1981): 224–45.

Reich, Charles A. *Greening of America: How the Youth Revolution Is Trying to Make America Livable*. New York: Random House, 1970.

Risco, Antonio. "Lo fantástico en un cuento de Julio Cortázar: 'Continuidad de los parques.'" In *Memoria del XX Congreso del Instituto Internacional de Literatura Iberoamericana*. Ed. Mátyás Horányi. Departamento de Español de la Universidad Eötvös Loránd de Budapest, 1982. 427–40.

Rodríguez Monegal, Emir. "Borges: Una teoría de la literatura fantástica." *Revista iberoamericana* 42.95 (1976): 177–89.

Roh, Franz. *Realismo mágico: Post expresionismo: Problemas de la pintura europea más reciento*. Trans. Fernando Vela. Madrid: Revista de Occidente, 1927. (Translation of *Nach-expressionismus, magischer realismus: Probleme der neusten europäischer Malerei*, 1925.)

Sartre, Jean-Paul. "Aminadab ou du fantastique considerée comme une langage." In *Critiques littéraires* (*Situations*, 1). Paris: Gallimard, 1975. 148–73.

Siebers, Tobin. *The Romantic Fantastic*. Ithaca: Cornell Univ. Press, 1984.

Sosnowski, Saúl. "Conocimiento, poético y aprensión racional de la realidad. . . ." In Helmy F. Giacoman, ed. *Homenaje a Julio Cortázar*. Long Island City: Las Américas, 1972. 427–44.

Todorov, Tzvetan, *The Fantastic: A Structural Approach to Literary Genre*. Trans. Richard Howard. Cleveland and London: The

Press of Western Reserve University, 1973.

——. *Introduction à la littérature fantastique.* Paris: Seuil, 1970.

——. "The Origin of Genres." *New Literary History* 8.1 (1976): 159–70.

——. *The Poetics of Prose.* Trans. Richard Howard. Ithaca: Cornell Univ. Press, 1977.

Updike, John. "Resisting the Big Guys." *The New Yorker* (August 24, 1987): 84.

Index of Authors Cited